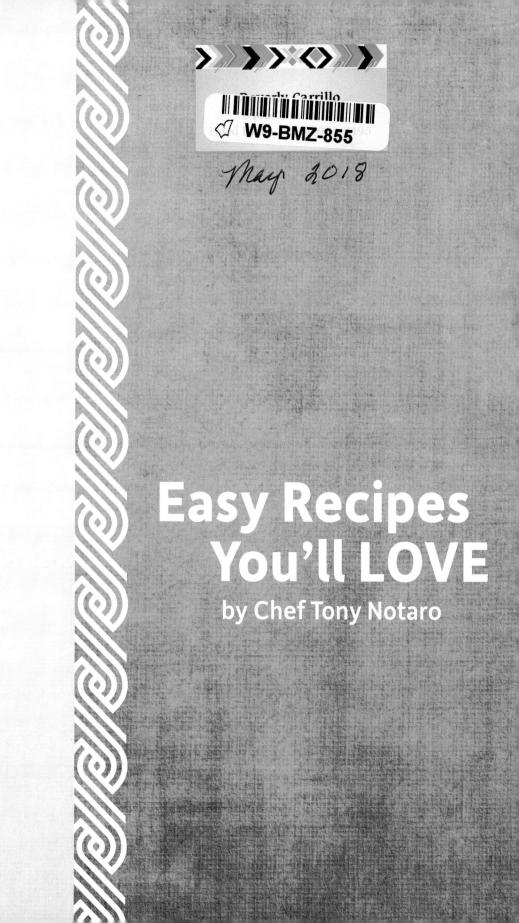

May 2018

Easy Recipes
You'll LOVE

by Chef Tony Notaro

Author, Chef Tony Notaro

Editors, Jodi Flayman, Merly Mesa, Carol Ginsburg

Recipe Development and Food Styling, Patty Rosenthal

Photographers, Victoria Krog, Kelly Rusin

Post Production, Hal Silverman of Hal Silverman Studio

Cover and Page Design, Lorraine Dan of Grand Design

The paper in this printing meets the requirements of the ANSI Standard Z39.48-1992.

While every care has been taken in compiling the recipes for this book, the publisher, Cogin, Inc., or any other person who has been involved in working on this publication assumes no responsibility or liability for any errors or omissions, inadvertent or not, that may be found in the recipes or text, nor for any problems or damages that may arise as a result of preparing these recipes.

If food allergies or dietary restrictions are a concern, it is recommended that you carefully read ingredient product labels as well as consult a nutritionist or your physician to determine if a particular recipe meets your dietary needs.

We encourage you to use caution when working with all kitchen equipment and to always follow food safety guidelines.

To purchase this book for business or promotional use or to purchase more than 50 copies at a discount, or for custom editions, please contact Cogin, Inc. at the address below.

Inquiries should be addressed to:

Cogin, Inc.

1770 NW 64 Street, Suite 500

Fort Lauderdale, FL 33309

ISBN: 978-0-9981635-3-6

Printed in the United States of America

First Edition

foreword

Many people have an appreciation for good food and enjoy a great meal. But it is rare when you find someone that also celebrates food and everything cooking involves. For me, that person is Chef Tony Notaro! During our more than 20-year friendship, we have demonstrated products on QVC®, cooked together, and of course, eaten together. We almost always chat about a new recipe we've tasted. So, when Chef Tony told me he was putting together a collection of his favorites in a new cookbook, my mouth began to water.

His book, *Easy Recipes You'll Love*, is a unique combination of dishes he grew up eating in his traditional Italian family, coupled with other menu-makers for people of all food backgrounds. Chef Tony takes an easy approach to these recipes, and you will quickly feel comfortable and confident in making delicious meals for your family. Plus, most of the recipes use ingredients you already have in your pantry or fridge.

The book takes you from breakfast and appetizers to salads and soups. I can't wait to try the Irish Cream French Toast, Pull Apart Bacon and Cheese Bread, and Love-in-a-Bowl Chicken Soup. Chef Tony includes lots of yummy poultry recipes, as well as a tribute to what he calls "Magnificent Meat!" Sign me up for Cheesy Ranch Chicken Bake and Family Sized Loaded Meatballs! He has seafood lovers and pasta aficionados covered, along with those looking for unique sides. And I can't forget his "To-Die-For Desserts!" and the S'mores Poke Cake. All in all, it's a smorgasbord of family-friendly foods that will delight everyone's taste buds.

With this fantastic book in your hands, you can dive in and experience the recipes Chef Tony has spent a lifetime perfecting and sharing. Use this as a guide to break free from the same meals we make over and over again. Before every show I host with Chef Tony, I always tell him, "I'll take good care of you today." Now, he's ready to return the favor and take each of you from the kitchen to the family dinner table. Every bite is a reminder to not only appreciate great food, but to also celebrate it. Thank you, Chef Tony, for all of the future Happy Dances!

Keep it flavorful,

David Venable
QVC Host, *In the Kitchen with David*®

introduction

When you're raised in a big Italian-American family, like I was, you quickly come to realize that family and food are everything. Even though both my parents were true-blooded Italians in every way, I grew up in a neighborhood that was as multicultural as it gets. Boy, am I grateful for that, since it not only introduced me to so many wonderful lifelong friends, but it offered me the opportunity to be exposed to a vast variety of food.

One thing I learned from watching my parents and my friends' parents cook as I grew up, was that they all added one ingredient that made everything taste better. (No, you won't find it in a bottle or buried in the produce section.) The ingredient was "love" and the only place you can find it is in your heart.

That's why the saying, "Taste the love... love the taste," is the inspiration behind this book and how I've been cooking all my life. In every occasion that I find myself in the kitchen – past, present, or future – I think of this. So, whether it's getting dinner on the table for the kids, having a few friends over for a meal, or sharing a feast with the whole family on special occasions (and let me tell you, we have a lot of those!), I never forget to add love.

There's nothing more I wish for than to be able to invite every single person who has ever watched me on TV or who has flipped through this book to come to my home for dinner. After all, that's what family does. Unfortunately, that's not possible, but my goal is to help you serve your family the very same quick and easy dishes that I would serve you.

My Crispy Chicken Fingers with Garlic Parm Sauce and Ham & Cheese Mac & Cheese are sure to be as popular with your family as they are with mine. And I can't wait for you to try my Old World Pasta Bolognese and Pop's Rice Stuffing, both recipes that have been part of my family forever. If you're a dessert lover, then you're in for a real sweet treat when you get a taste of my Special Occasion Cannoli Cake and Secret Ingredient Fabulous Flan; they're personal favorites.

As someone with a busy schedule, I know how important it is to be able to easily put dinner on the table every night of the week. That's why all of the recipes in this cookbook use off-the-shelf ingredients and have simple step-by-step instructions. These recipes are simple, family taste-tested, and memorable. I truly hope you have as much fun and joy cooking from this book as I did creating it for you.

Many Blessings & Happy Cookin'

Chef Tony

table of contents

dedication

This book is dedicated with great pride to my mother Jeana, who was, is, and always will be my greatest inspiration and the driving force behind my cooking career; Papa Frank, who was the rock and patriarch of our family and instilled in me that family always comes first; and Mama Jeanie, who showed me that when you add love to a dish, you can always taste the difference.

Frank & Jeana (a.k.a. Papa & Mom)

I also want to thank Vivian, our children, and grandchildren for their undying support and love—without you I have nothing. You are all the wind in my sails. And thank you to all of my mentors, chefs, life coaches, and my Sensei... all of the people who have loved and supported me throughout my life, and continue to do so. This book would not be possible without all of you. You know who you are and I thank you from the bottom of my heart.

One last mention to those of you who work in the culinary arts, but never had formal training. Like me, you learned this art the hands-on way... on the line, in the trenches! BRAVO to YOU! You are truly my heroes!

a little bit about chef tony

Anthony Joseph Notaro ("Chef Tony") has spent the majority of his life working with food. From helping out in his grandmother's Southern Italian restaurant as a child, to demonstrating unique kitchen products in adulthood, Chef Tony has proven that cooking is his lifelong passion. Some may even argue that it's in his blood – his mother owned a home-based Italian catering business while his father sold fresh produce.

At 18, Chef Tony ventured into the world of culinary demonstrations, eventually coming up with the idea to promote his own recipes alongside the products he helped to market. His authenticity and trustworthiness as a presenter paved the way for even more growth. Along with endorsing and marketing several successful brands, he is a regular guest on QVC, and has his own brand of food and kitchen products.

Chef Tony truly believes that anyone can cook, given the right tools and guidance. This personal philosophy is the reason why he's ready to share his love for cooking through this new cookbook that features many of his favorite easy recipes.

"We were poor growing up. Whatever was left over from the night before went into omelets in the morning. Those were the best omelets."

rise & shine breakfasts

all-in-one breakfast pizzas

Makes 4

My mom always had dough on hand, and sometimes she'd surprise us with pizza for breakfast. Instead of a standard pie, she'd make it breakfast-friendly by topping it with bacon and eggs. I loved this so much as a kid that I kept the tradition going. Now, I make these personal-sized, all-in-one, breakfast pizzas for my family and, let me tell you, nobody ever complains.

1 pound bakery pizza dough, cut into quarters

1 cup shredded mozzarella cheese, divided

1 cup marinara sauce, divided

8 eggs

8 slices crispy-cooked bacon, coarsely crumbled

Fresh basil, slivered

1 tablespoon grated Parmesan cheese (optional)

✳ Preheat oven to 450 degrees F. Brush 2 baking sheets with olive oil.

✳ Using a floured rolling pin or your hands, roll out or shape each piece of dough into an 8-inch circle, and place on baking sheets. (Don't worry if they aren't perfectly round!)

✳ Sprinkle each piece of dough with ¼ cup of the cheese and top that with a ¼ cup of the sauce. (Yes, the sauce goes over the cheese.) Crack 2 eggs on top of each pizza.

✳ Bake 10 to 12 minutes or until the crust is crispy and the eggs are cooked to your desired doneness. Evenly sprinkle the cooked bacon, slivered basil, and Parmesan cheese, if desired, over each pizza and serve.

Chef Tony's Tip: Change these up using whatever you have on hand! Sometimes I swap out the bacon for prosciutto or use leftover cooked sausage that's been crumbled or cut into thin slices.

fresh
spring frittata

Serves 6-8

Growing up, Dad was the produce guy. He sold fresh produce his whole life, which meant that we were a family that ate a lot of greens. One of my favorite ways to use greens, and any other veggies, is to toss them into a frittata. Frittatas are easy and good for serving a lot of hungry people sitting around a breakfast table. In this version, I use fresh asparagus and sliced scallions to add a special springtime touch.

10 eggs

½ cup honey Dijon salad dressing

2 tablespoons grated Parmesan cheese, plus extra for garnish

½ teaspoon salt

¼ teaspoon black pepper

1 tablespoon butter

1 tablespoon olive oil

½ pound fresh asparagus, trimmed and cut into ½-inch pieces

½ cup sliced scallions

¼ cup roasted red peppers, drained, diced

2 cups fresh baby spinach

❋ In a large bowl, combine eggs, salad dressing, 2 tablespoons Parmesan cheese, the salt, and pepper; mix well and set aside.

❋ In a 10-inch skillet over medium-high heat, melt the butter with the oil. Add asparagus, scallions, and red peppers, and sauté 5 minutes until almost tender. Add spinach, give it a good toss, and cook until it begins to wilt.

❋ Pour egg mixture over vegetables and stir until everything is evenly mixed. Cover the skillet, reduce heat to low, and cook 15 to 20 minutes or until the eggs are set.

❋ Place a large dinner plate over the frittata and carefully flip it onto the plate. Sprinkle with additional Parmesan cheese before cutting it into pie-shaped wedges. Serve immediately.

meat lover's cheese omelet

Serves 2-3

I love omelets - always have and always will. When my family was going through hard times, they were a favorite; we would just take whatever we had left over in the fridge and put it into our omelets. These days, I love to experiment with new combinations. In this one, I kept it simple and really tasty by adding in lots of ham, sausage, and cheese.

1 teaspoon olive oil

¼ cup cooked crumbled sausage

¼ cup diced cooked ham

2 tablespoons chopped onion

6 eggs, beaten

½ cup shredded cheddar cheese, divided

✳ In a 10-inch skillet over medium heat, heat oil until hot. Add sausage, ham, and onion. Sauté 3 to 4 minutes or until heated through. Remove from skillet and set aside.

✳ Add eggs to skillet and gently stir for 1 minute; stop stirring and allow egg to set up (this will take about 1 minute). Top the eggs with the meat mixture and sprinkle with ¼ cup of cheese.

✳ As you slide the omelet out of the pan, gently fold it in half. Sprinkle the top with remaining cheese, and serve.

Chef Tony's Tip: Go ahead and try this with some different cheeses! I've made variations of this omelet using everything from American cheese to gruyère. As for the ham, I typically buy it from the deli, have them cut it into slices about ¼-inch thick, and then dice it at home.

steakhouse eggs benedict

Serves 2-4

Friends, this is the breakfast you might want to serve your spouse when you want to talk them into planning a vacation! In all seriousness, I love this fancied-up way of making eggs Benedict. Saturdays are typically "steak night" at my house, so we've been known to save some steak to make these on Sundays after church. And instead of the traditional Hollandaise sauce, I've found that Béarnaise sauce complements the steak beautifully.

1 tablespoon butter

1 (8-ounce) filet mignon, cut into 4 equal slices

$\frac{1}{8}$ teaspoon salt

$\frac{1}{8}$ teaspoon black pepper

6 medium-thick stalks asparagus, trimmed and cut in half crosswise

$\frac{1}{4}$ cup white vinegar

4 eggs

2 English muffins, split in half

1 (.9-ounce) packet Béarnaise sauce, prepared according to package directions

✺ In a large skillet over medium-high heat, melt the butter. Sprinkle each filet slice evenly with salt and pepper and cook 1 to 2 minutes per side or until desired doneness. Remove from heat and cover to keep warm. (Remember that these will continue to cook after removing them from the heat, so make sure you don't overcook them.)

✺ Meanwhile, fill a large saucepan $\frac{2}{3}$ of the way with water and, over high heat, bring to a boil. Add the asparagus and cook until tender-crisp. (This will take about 5 minutes.) Remove asparagus to a paper towel-lined plate; set aside.

✺ Reduce heat to low and add vinegar to the water. Gently crack eggs, one at a time, into the simmering water. Cook 4 to 6 minutes or until the eggs are firm on the outside and the yolk is cooked just like you like it.

✺ Meanwhile, toast the English muffins. Place the English muffin halves on a platter and top each half with a slice of filet mignon. Top each half with 3 pieces of asparagus (as shown) and, using a slotted spoon, place an egg on top of the asparagus. Spoon warm Béarnaise sauce over top, and enjoy.

heavenly homemade hash

Serves 4-6

Turn a basic breakfast into something special with this recipe for a heavenly homemade hash. This is a great way to use up leftover, cooked corned beef or you could get some corned beef cut extra-thick at the deli, and dice it at home.

1 stick butter

2 onions, diced

3 cups refrigerated diced potatoes

¼ teaspoon salt

¼ teaspoon black pepper

3 cups diced cooked corned beef (about 1 pound)

✸ In a large skillet over medium-high heat, melt the butter; sauté the onions 3 to 4 minutes or until tender.

✸ Add the potatoes, salt, and pepper and cook 10 to 12 minutes, stirring occasionally. Add the corned beef and continue to cook until the potatoes and corned beef start to get crispy.

Chef Tony's Tip: If you want to spice things up, add in a chopped jalapeño pepper along with the onions. Oh, and I've been known to serve this with two poached eggs, and let the yolks ooze into the hash. Oh my gosh!

very veggie hash browns

Serves 6-8

I love me some hash browns, and they're even better when you load them up with flavorful veggies, which is exactly what I do. Not only do they add great taste to this dish, but they also add some nutrition and color. This is worthy of being served at breakfast or dinner!

¼ cup olive oil

1 (2-pound) package frozen cubed hash brown potatoes

1 red bell pepper, chopped

1 onion, chopped

2 cups sliced fresh mushrooms

1 teaspoon salt

½ teaspoon black pepper

✹ In a large skillet over high heat, heat oil until hot. Add the potatoes and cook 10 to 12 minutes or until lightly browned.

✹ Add bell pepper, onion, mushrooms, salt, and black pepper. Cook 6 to 8 minutes or until vegetables are tender, stirring occasionally.

Chef Tony's Tip: I've sold quite a few mandolines and hand-held choppers over the years, and I've always said, they're a blessing for recipes like this (since you need to chop and slice a few different veggies). So, if you have one in your kitchen, this is the time to put it to use!

bagels & lox breakfast bake

Serves 4-5

Being from Brooklyn, I was raised on bagels and lox - I eat it at least twice a week. But if you've never been, all you have to do is eat this dish, and it's like you're there. This one's a good one to make for the family, especially since you can prepare it the night before and bake it in the morning.

2 to 3 large "everything" bagels, cut into 2-inch chunks

2 tablespoons butter, melted

5 eggs

1-½ cups milk

4 ounces smoked salmon, diced

4 ounces cream cheese, cut into cubes

2 tablespoons chopped red onion

❋ Preheat oven to 350 degrees F. Coat an 8-inch square baking dish with cooking spray. Place the bagel chunks in the baking dish. (If "everything" bagels aren't your favorite, go ahead and use whatever you like best. I do suggest that you stay away from sweet bagels like cinnamon raisin and blueberry, since they won't pair well with the other ingredients in this dish.)

❋ In a large bowl, whisk butter, eggs, and milk. Stir in salmon and cream cheese. Pour egg mixture over bagels.

❋ Cover and bake 20 minutes. Remove cover and continue baking 10 to 15 minutes or until the center is set. Sprinkle with onions, and serve.

Chef Tony's Tip: After this comes out of the oven, I like to top it with some sliced fresh chives and pickled capers. It adds a nice finishing touch to this mouthwatering bake.

4-ingredient breakfast roll-ups

Makes 16

Not every morning calls for something as fancy as Steakhouse Eggs Benedict (page 6) or something from scratch like Bacon-Studded Waffles (page 19). When I want to keep things real simple, I make these 4-ingredient roll-ups. They're easy and really satisfying. Plus, they're just as good for a late-night snack as they are for helping me rise and shine.

1 (16-ounce) package bulk pork breakfast sausage

½ red bell pepper, diced

4 scallions, thinly sliced

2 (8-ounce) packages refrigerated crescent rolls (8 rolls each)

❁ Preheat oven to 400 degrees F. In a medium bowl, combine sausage, red pepper, and scallions; mix well.

❁ Unroll 1 package of crescent rolls and using your fingers, pinch the seams together to create one large rectangle. Repeat with the second package of crescent rolls. Spread half of the sausage mixture evenly over each rectangle.

❁ Starting from the narrow end, roll up jelly roll-style. Cut each roll into 8 equal slices and place each on its side on a rimmed baking sheet.

❁ Bake 25 to 30 minutes or until sausage is no longer pink and crust is golden. Serve warm.

Chef Tony's Tip: These are really good with a side of mustard for dipping. The mustard can be spicy or sweet, depending on your preference.

slow cooker cran-apple oatmeal

Serves 3-4

You'll be thinking of cool autumn days when you make this slow cooker oatmeal. It's full of the flavors of the season, which means that you can expect the smells of apple, cinnamon, and maple to fill your home with their inviting aroma. Cozying up to a bowl of this oatmeal is just one of the many things I look forward to each year.

2 apples, peeled, cored, and chopped

1-½ cups water

1-½ cups milk

1 cup steel-cut oats

½ cup coarsely chopped walnuts

½ cup dried cranberries

2 tablespoons butter, cut into pieces

2 tablespoons maple syrup

½ teaspoon ground cinnamon

¼ teaspoon salt

❋ Coat a 3-quart or larger slow cooker with cooking spray.

❋ Place apples, water, milk, oats, walnuts, cranberries and butter in the slow cooker; stir well.

❋ In a small bowl, combine the maple syrup, cinnamon, and salt; mix well. Pour into the slow cooker and stir until everything is well combined.

❋ Cover and cook on HIGH 2 hours or on LOW 4 hours, or to desired consistency. (If it looks like it's getting too thick for your taste, simply add a bit more water or some apple cider until it's the consistency you like.)

Chef Tony's Tip: If you're making this for company, I suggest serving it "buffet style" right from the slow cooker with a selection of different toppings, so that everyone can customize their own bowl.

grab & go
breakfast sliders

Makes 12

We all get a little busy at times. For me, there are days when I've got a lot going on at QVC or when the family needs me to get some things done. I don't like skipping meals, so whenever I know that I've got an extra-busy day coming up, I prepare these breakfast sliders the day before. Then when I'm rushing out the door, I can just grab a couple, heat them up, and go!

1 stick butter, melted, divided

2 tablespoons brown sugar

2 tablespoon yellow mustard

1 (12-count) package dinner-size Hawaiian sweet rolls

12 slices provolone cheese

8 eggs, scrambled

6 slices deli ham

1 tablespoon grated Parmesan cheese

✸ Preheat oven to 350 degrees F. In a small bowl, combine 7 tablespoons of melted butter, the brown sugar, and mustard; mix well.

✸ Place the package of rolls on the counter and, using a serrated knife, cut the rolls in half, horizontally. (Do not separate into individual rolls.) Spread the brown sugar mixture evenly over both cut sides of the rolls. Place the bottom half in a 9- x 13-inch baking dish.

✸ Place 4 slices of provolone cheese over the cut side of the rolls in the baking dish, and top with scrambled eggs. Place 4 more slices of cheese, the ham, and remaining 4 slices of provolone cheese over that. Place top of rolls over the filling, and brush the tops of rolls with remaining melted butter. Sprinkle with Parmesan cheese.

✸ Bake 12 to 15 minutes or until cheese is melted and the filling is piping hot. Cut into individual sandwiches.

peach melba dutch pancake

Serves 4-6

These puffy pancakes always take my breath away. They're impressive to look at, they're easy to make, and they taste phenomenal. You can serve this for brunch with the family, as a sort of "breakfast for dessert" kind of treat. It will surely please anyone with a sweet tooth at your table.

1 stick butter, divided

6 eggs

1 cup milk

½ teaspoon salt

1 cup all-purpose flour

½ cup light brown sugar

6 peaches, peeled and thinly sliced

½ cup raspberries

Frozen whipped topping, thawed, for garnish

Powdered sugar for sprinkling

✳ Preheat oven to 425 degrees F. Place 6 tablespoons (¾ stick) butter into a 9- x 13-inch baking dish; place in oven to melt. Once butter is melted, remove baking dish from oven, making sure butter has evenly coated bottom of pan.

✳ Meanwhile, in a blender, combine eggs, milk, and salt; blend until frothy. Slowly add flour, mixing until well blended. Pour the egg mixture into the hot baking dish.

✳ Bake 25 to 30 minutes or until golden brown and the center is set. (Don't be alarmed when the edges have puffed up and the center is flatter. That's the way it should be!)

✳ While that's baking, in a skillet over medium heat, melt remaining 2 tablespoons butter. Add brown sugar and peaches and sauté 1 to 2 minutes or until tender. Gently, stir in raspberries. Spoon peach mixture over pancake, garnish with whipped topping, and sprinkle with powdered sugar. Serve immediately.

Chef Tony's Tip: Since I like using the freshest produce possible, this recipe is perfect for the summer, when peaches are at their peak. When peach season turns into apple season, you can bet that I replace the peaches with fresh apples and substitute the raspberries with dried cranberries.

classic
buttermilk pancakes

Serves 3-4

I keep things pretty simple with these pancakes, and I think that you'll love them all the more because of it. Since they're made with buttermilk, they're lighter and fluffier than your average pancake. Plus, they make a great base for all of your favorite toppings, so you can sprinkle on the chocolate chips, serve with a side of fresh fruit, or top with cold maple syrup (my favorite!).

2 cups all-purpose flour

⅓ cup sugar

2 teaspoons baking powder

½ teaspoon baking soda

½ teaspoon salt

2 eggs

2 cups buttermilk

2 tablespoons butter, melted, plus extra butter for cooking

✲ In a large bowl, combine flour, sugar, baking powder, baking soda, and salt; mix well. In a medium bowl, beat eggs, buttermilk, and 2 tablespoons of melted butter; stir into dry ingredients just until combined. (Be careful not to overmix or your pancakes will have lots of air bubbles.)

✲ On a griddle pan or in a large skillet over medium heat, melt 1 tablespoon butter. Pour about ⅓ cup of batter onto griddle. Cook 2 to 3 minutes or until bubbles begin to form, then turn over and cook an additional 2 minutes or until golden brown.

✲ Set cooked pancakes on a baking sheet and place in a warm oven (200 degrees F) to keep warm while you make the rest of the pancakes. Repeat with the remaining batter, adding more butter as needed.

Chef Tony's Tip: If you don't have buttermilk, you can add 2 tablespoons of either white vinegar or cream of tartar to 2 cups of milk; stir and let sit about 5 minutes, then use in place of buttermilk.

irish cream french toast

Serves 3-4

French toast has always been a special breakfast in my house. My mom made it, I make it, and now that my kids are older, they make it too. It's like a holiday thing you make on non-holidays (if you get what I mean). I add a little Irish cream to my milk mixture, since it adds such a nice spirited flavor.

6 eggs

½ cup milk

½ cup plus 2 tablespoons Irish cream liqueur, divided

1 teaspoon vanilla extract

1 tablespoon sugar

1 teaspoon ground cinnamon

1 loaf challah (egg bread), cut into 6 (1-inch-thick) slices

2 tablespoons butter

½ cup maple syrup

✵ In a shallow dish, whisk the eggs, milk, ½ cup liqueur, the vanilla, sugar, and cinnamon. Dip the bread in the egg mixture, letting it soak about 3 seconds on each side. (If you soak it too long, it'll be mushy, and if you don't soak it long enough, it'll be dry.)

✵ Heat a griddle pan or large skillet over medium heat. Place 1 tablespoon of the butter on the skillet and, when it melts, place the bread onto the griddle and cook 1 to 2 minutes on each side or until golden brown. Remove to a plate and cover to keep warm. Repeat with remaining bread, adding more butter as needed.

✵ Meanwhile, in a small bowl, combine syrup and remaining 2 tablespoons liqueur; mix well. Cut each slice of French toast in half, diagonally, and serve with syrup mixture.

Chef Tony's Tip: If you can't find challah, I suggest picking up a loaf of homestyle white bread or even a nutty raisin bread. The most important thing is to get a whole loaf that you can cut into thick slices yourself.

bacon-studded waffles

Makes 6

I love waffles - all kinds of waffles. And I love to put bacon in my waffle batter; it just makes sense to me. A little sweet, a little savory, a little smoky; you just can't go wrong. While mixes are nice, sometimes there's nothing better than starting from scratch. Once you get a taste of these, I'm sure you'll agree. As for the toppings, let's just say I like a little waffles with my butter.

2 cups all-purpose flour
3 tablespoons sugar
1 teaspoon baking powder
1 teaspoon baking soda
½ teaspoon salt
2 eggs, beaten
2 cups buttermilk
½ stick butter, melted
1 teaspoon vanilla extract
½ cup bacon pieces

❁ Preheat an electric waffle iron according to directions. Coat with cooking spray.

❁ In a large bowl, combine flour, sugar, baking powder, baking soda, and salt. Stir in remaining ingredients; mix well.

❁ Using a ½ cup measure (or whatever amount suggested by your waffle maker's instructions), pour batter into bottom of waffle iron. Close lid and cook 60 to 90 seconds or until golden. Using a fork, carefully remove waffle to a plate; cover to keep warm. Repeat with remaining batter. Serve immediately.

Chef Tony's Tip: To make sure that the bacon is evenly distributed in all of the waffles, give the batter a quick stir before pouring it into the waffle maker. This will ensure that any bacon that fell to the bottom of the bowl while it sat, gets evenly mixed into the batter.

choco-chunk muffins

Makes 12

Muffins make for marvelous mornings, especially when they're loaded up with lots of chocolate chunks, like mine are. Instead of making a stop at the bakery for some breakfast treats, I suggest giving these muffins a try. They're perfect for a special brunch or for sharing with those you love.

1 stick butter, softened

1-¼ cups sugar

2 eggs

2 cups all-purpose flour

2 teaspoons baking powder

½ teaspoon salt

½ cup milk

1 teaspoon vanilla extract

1 (12-ounce) package semi-sweet chocolate chunks

2 tablespoons coarse sugar for sprinkling

✳ Preheat oven to 375 degrees F. Line 12 muffin cups with paper liners.

✳ In a large bowl, using an electric mixer on medium speed, beat butter and sugar until creamy. Add eggs, one at a time, beating well after each addition. (Make sure you add the eggs one at a time as it makes the muffins fluffier.) Then add flour, baking powder, and salt; beat well. Add milk and vanilla, and beat until thoroughly combined.

✳ Fold the chocolate chunks into the batter and fill each muffin cup ¾ full. Sprinkle the batter evenly with coarse sugar.

✳ Bake 23 to 27 minutes or until a toothpick comes out clean. Remove the muffins from the pan, and allow to cool before enjoying.

Chef Tony's Tip: You can turn these into bite-sized muffins by baking them in a mini muffin pan or make huge ones with a large muffin pan. If you do change the size, make sure you adjust the baking time as well. You can tell when they're done when a toothpick inserted in the center comes out clean.

cinnamon bun pull-apart bread

Serves 4-6

This bread has what I like to call a "come and get it" aroma to it. If you aren't getting up to your alarm, you're getting up for a chance to pull apart a piece of this amazing bread. With this recipe, you'll experience all of the flavors and smells of a cinnamon bun, in a fun and easy-to-share loaf. Just make sure that everyone knows that it's supposed to be shared or someone in the family might make it disappear all on their own.

3 tablespoons butter, melted

1 teaspoon vanilla extract

3 tablespoons brown sugar

1 tablespoon granulated sugar

1 teaspoon ground cinnamon

1 (16.3-ounce) package refrigerated buttermilk biscuits (8 biscuits)

Glaze

1 tablespoon milk

1 tablespoon butter, melted

½ teaspoon vanilla extract

¾ cup powdered sugar

✳ Preheat oven to 350 degrees F. Coat a 9- x 5-inch loaf pan with cooking spray and set aside.

✳ In a small bowl, mix together 3 tablespoons of butter and 1 teaspoon of vanilla. In another small bowl, combine the brown sugar, granulated sugar, and cinnamon; mix well.

✳ Separate the dough into 8 biscuits. With your fingers, separate each biscuit into 2 layers, making a total of 16 biscuit rounds. Brush one side of each biscuit with the butter mixture, and sprinkle with a teaspoon of the sugar mixture. (You should have some of each left over.)

✳ Stack biscuits in 4 piles, each with 4 biscuits. Place each stack on its side, end to end, in the loaf pan. Make sure that the sides of the biscuits that touch the ends of the pan are not buttered and sugared or they will stick to the pan. Brush the top of the loaf with the remaining butter mixture and sprinkle with the remaining sugar mixture.

✳ Bake 25 to 30 minutes or until golden and biscuits are cooked through. Remove from oven and allow to cool in pan for 2 minutes. Using a spatula, remove from pan to a serving platter.

✳ Meanwhile, to make Glaze, in a small bowl, mix milk, 1 tablespoon butter, and ½ teaspoon vanilla. Add powdered sugar and whisk until smooth. Drizzle over bread and serve warm.

"There are times I've been told there's nothing in the house to eat. I can look at what's on hand and create an incredible meal out of almost nothing!!!"

amazing appetizers

pull-apart bacon & cheese bread

Serves 6-8

Whenever I serve this one, I make sure that everyone knows the rules – there are none. This is a dive-in finger food, where you get to pick the piece you want. (As for me, I look for the ooey-gooiest pieces!) I like to introduce it as a cross between a grilled cheese and a twist on garlic bread. You get so much more than what you could've imagined – like three amazing cheeses and lots of smoky bacon.

1 round loaf hearty white or sourdough bread, unsliced

4 ounces cream cheese, softened

½ cup mayonnaise

1 teaspoon garlic powder

2 cups shredded cheddar cheese

2 cups shredded mozzarella cheese

¼ cup real bacon pieces

¼ cup chopped scallion

✱ Preheat oven to 375 degrees F. Tear a piece of aluminum foil large enough to loosely wrap the whole bread.

✱ Using a serrated knife, make a series of parallel cuts in the bread about 1-inch apart, and about 2-inches deep. Then, rotate the bread and cut it until you end up with a crisscross pattern. (Check out the photo for a better idea of what I mean – it's really easy! To make it even easier, I like to use my Miracle Blade All Purpose Slicer.) Place the bread on the foil, and set aside.

✱ In a medium bowl, combine remaining ingredients; mix well. Evenly spread cheese mixture into all of the bread cuts, being careful not to break the bread apart. (This can get a little messy, but it's worth the effort.) If you get some of the cheese filling on the crust, wipe it off with a paper towel. Then, wrap the bread loosely in foil.

✱ Place the wrapped loaf on a baking sheet and bake for 15 minutes, then uncover it, and continue to bake for 10 to 15 minutes or until the cheese is melted. Serve warm.

Chef Tony's Tip: Finding the right bread is key here. You want a bread that has a nice firm crust, with a soft and spongy texture inside (to complement the cheesy filling).

Amazing Appetizers

buffalo chicken skewers

Makes 12

I like traditional Buffalo wings as much as anyone else, but when I'm making them for a party, I like to serve them up this way instead. There are a few things that make these better for guests: they're healthier (because they're "grilled"), they're easier to eat (because there are no bones to deal with), and they have just the right amount of heat to them.

3 (4-ounce) boneless, skinless chicken breasts, cut into 12 strips

12 (6-inch) wooden skewers

¼ cup hot cayenne pepper sauce (also known as wing sauce)

1 tablespoon butter, melted

Blue Cheese Dressing

¾ cup sour cream

¼ cup mayonnaise

1-½ teaspoons white vinegar

⅛ teaspoon salt

⅛ teaspoon black pepper

4 ounces crumbled blue cheese

Celery sticks

❊ Weave the chicken strips onto the skewers and place them on a platter.

❊ In a small bowl, combine cayenne pepper sauce and butter. Brush this mixture evenly over the chicken until it's completely coated.

❊ Coat a grill pan with cooking spray and heat over medium heat until hot. Place chicken on grill pan and cook 6 to 8 minutes or until chicken is no longer pink, turning occasionally.

❊ Meanwhile, in a medium bowl, combine Blue Cheese Dressing ingredients, except blue cheese; mix well, then stir in blue cheese. Refrigerate until ready to use.

❊ Serve chicken skewers with celery sticks and Blue Cheese Dressing.

Chef Tony's Tip: If you want to throw these on the grill, make sure you soak the skewers in cold water for at least 15 minutes before weaving the chicken strips onto them. This will prevent the skewers from burning while the chicken cooks.

Amazing Appetizers

throw-together pepperoni pizza puffs

Makes 10

We're a pizza-loving family, which means we've come up with some great ways to serve pizza for practically every meal (just check out my All-in-One Breakfast Pizzas on page 2). These pizza puffs are great for those times when somebody drops in unexpectedly or when one of my grandkids wants a fun snack. Since I don't know anyone who doesn't like pizza, these are always a guaranteed winner.

1 (7.5-ounce) package refrigerated biscuits (10 biscuits)

Garlic powder for sprinkling

3 (1-ounce) mozzarella string cheese sticks, cut into 1-inch pieces

2 tablespoons chopped pepperoni slices

Cooking Spray

½ cup pizza or spaghetti sauce

✺ Preheat oven to 375 degrees F. Coat a baking sheet with cooking spray.

✺ Separate biscuit dough into 10 pieces. Using your thumb, make an indentation in the center of each biscuit. Lightly sprinkle each one with garlic powder, then top with a piece of cheese and a few pieces of pepperoni.

✺ Gently stretch the dough over filling, making sure you cover filling completely, and pinching the dough to secure it. Place seam-side down on baking sheet and spray the tops of each puff with cooking spray, so that they end up with a nice golden color.

✺ Bake for 10 to 12 minutes or until golden. Serve warm with sauce for dipping, and let the party begin.

Chef Tony's Tip: You can make these with cooked sausage or any of your favorite pizza fillings. Just make sure you chop everything up small, so that you can still wrap the dough around it.

antipasto on a stick

Makes 12

In my house, "antipasto" was always translated as "wake up the appetite." We make antipasto to get the taste buds going in preparation for the meal that's to come. This is a fun way to serve this traditional Italian appetizer. You'll notice I call for two different types of olives — that's because each one adds its own unique flavor and look to these.

12 (6-inch) skewers

12 large pitted Kalamata olives

12 mini sweet yellow peppers

2 (½-inch-thick) salami slices, cut into 24 chunks

12 small balls of fresh mozzarella cheese (see Tip)

12 cherry tomatoes

12 large pitted green olives

Old World Vinaigrette

½ cup olive oil

¼ cup red wine vinegar

1 teaspoon lemon juice

1 teaspoon dried oregano

½ teaspoon salt

¼ teaspoon black pepper

✳ On each skewer, alternately thread 1 Kalamata olive, 1 sweet pepper, 1 salami chunk, 1 mozzarella cheese ball, 1 cherry tomato, another salami chunk, and 1 green olive. Place skewers on a serving platter or in a 9- x 13-inch baking dish.

✳ In a medium bowl, whisk Old World Vinaigrette ingredients until well combined. When ready to serve, drizzle the dressing over the skewers. (You can make these up to a day ahead of time. The dressing will soak into the antipasto and make it extra flavorful.)

Chef Tony's Tip: If your grocery store is out of the fresh mozzarella that comes in small balls, just go ahead and buy the larger ball. Then cut it into 1-½-inch chunks. Or you could always substitute chunks of provolone cheese from the deli for a different flavor.

party-perfect stuffed baked brie

Serves 6-8

You want to add a little pizzazz to your party? Put this Brie on the table. I'm telling you, this Brie is really special. I usually make it with fig jam, because it's one of my favorites, but sometimes I use sour cherry or raspberry jam instead. When people first take a look at this, they just grab a small piece for a taste, but then... I notice that they keep going back for more and more. It's addictive.

1 (8-ounce) container refrigerated crescent rolls

1 (8-ounce) round Brie cheese

3 tablespoons fig jam

2 tablespoons chopped pecans

1 egg, beaten

❋ Preheat oven to 350 degrees F. Coat a baking sheet with cooking spray.

❋ Unroll crescent roll dough and pinch together at perforations to create one big sheet.

❋ Cut the Brie in half horizontally, and place one half, cut-side up on the center of the dough. Spread fig jam over that half of the Brie; sprinkle with pecans. Place the other half, cut-side down on top of the pecans. (This is like making a sandwich.) Wrap the dough up over the top of the Brie and pinch it firmly to seal.

❋ Place seam-side down on the baking sheet and brush with beaten egg. Bake for 25 to 30 minutes or until golden. Allow to cool slightly before serving. Place on a cutting board and serve while still warm.

Chef Tony's Tip: Make sure you let this rest for 5 to 10 minutes before cutting into it, so that the cheese doesn't ooze all over the cutting board. You can also use a sheet of defrosted puff pastry dough instead of the crescent rolls, just to change it up.

crab shack stuffed mushrooms

Serves 6-8

Ok, y'all know I'm all about being real – for me, crab stuffed mushrooms are all about the crab. The mushroom is really just the vehicle that holds the crab. So, I splurge on the lump crabmeat. Yes, it's a little more expensive, but it makes these taste really special. Anyway, these aren't an everyday treat, so it's okay to go all out!

1 pound large fresh mushrooms

4 tablespoons butter, divided

¼ cup plus 2 tablespoons bread crumbs

4 ounces (about ½ cup) lump crabmeat

¼ teaspoon seafood seasoning

¼ teaspoon onion powder

⅛ teaspoon salt

⅛ teaspoon black pepper

✵ Preheat oven to 375 degrees F. Gently clean the mushrooms by wiping them with a damp paper towel. (If you wash them under running water they can get mushy.)

✵ Remove the stems from ¾ of the best looking mushrooms, and set aside the caps. Finely chop the mushroom stems and the remaining ¼ of the whole mushrooms.

✵ In a large skillet over medium heat, melt 3 tablespoons butter. Add chopped mushrooms, and cook 4 to 5 minutes or until tender. Remove from heat and add ¼ cup bread crumbs, the crabmeat, seafood seasoning, onion powder, salt, and pepper; mix gently so that you don't break up the crab chunks.

✵ Using a teaspoon, stuff the mushroom caps with the crab mixture and place on an ungreased, rimmed baking sheet. In a small bowl, melt remaining 1 tablespoon butter. Add remaining 2 tablespoons bread crumbs; mix well. Sprinkle that mixture evenly over the tops of the mushroom caps, and right before serving, bake 15 to 18 minutes or until heated through.

Chef Tony's Tip: If you want to give these an even richer taste, you can swap out the bread crumbs with crushed buttery crackers.

my cheese-filled rice balls

Makes 20

In Italian, these are called "arancini," and I make these for special occasions – Easter, Christmas, birthdays, you name it. Although there's some work involved in making these, they're well worth it. You can make these larger if you want to serve them as a main course, and you can even start with cooked, leftover rice (like my Mom did). The cheesy center is a tasty surprise!

2 cups chicken broth

1 cup Arborio rice (see Tip)

2 eggs

⅓ cup grated Parmesan cheese

1 tablespoon chopped fresh parsley

1 teaspoon garlic powder

¼ teaspoon salt

¼ teaspoon black pepper

¾ cup bread crumbs

4 ounces mozzarella cheese, cut into 20 (1-inch) cubes

1-½ cups vegetable oil

✳ In a medium saucepan over high heat, bring chicken broth to a boil; stir in rice, cover, and reduce heat to low. Cook 15 to 18 minutes or until liquid is absorbed.

✳ Meanwhile, in a bowl, whisk eggs, Parmesan cheese, parsley, garlic powder, salt, and pepper. Remove rice from heat, allow to cool, and slowly pour the egg mixture into the rice, stirring constantly to prevent the egg from cooking until it's thoroughly combined. Refrigerate this mixture for 1 hour.

✳ Place bread crumbs in a shallow dish. Remove chilled rice from the refrigerator and, using your hands, form the rice mixture into 20 (1-inch) balls. (Make sure your hands are wet to prevent the rice from sticking to them.) Make an indentation in each ball and place a piece of mozzarella in it, then cover with the rice mixture. (This is important so that the cheese won't ooze out while it cooks.) Roll each rice ball in the bread crumbs until evenly coated.

✳ In a large deep skillet over medium heat, heat oil until hot, but not smoking. Fry rice balls in batches, 4 to 5 minutes or until golden, turning occasionally. Drain on paper towels and serve warm.

Chef Tony's Tip: Arborio rice is a short-grained sticky rice. It's the best rice for making arancini because it helps these keep their shape. If time permits, I like to refrigerate the breaded rice balls for 20 to 30 minutes before frying, which also helps them hold up nicely.

asian-glazed chicken wings

Serves 6-8

When I lived in Las Vegas, I entertained quite a lot. I found out pretty early on, one of the things that people like most is something they're familiar with – like chicken wings. So, I gave them what they wanted, but with a twist. These chicken wings combine my love for Asian flavors with a tried-and-true American favorite. You're going to love them.

4 pounds split chicken wings or drumettes, thawed if frozen

1 cup sweet and sour sauce

½ cup honey

¼ cup Thai sweet chili sauce (see Tip)

1 tablespoon soy sauce

3 cloves garlic, chopped

1 teaspoon ground ginger

1-½ tablespoons sesame seeds

✳ Preheat oven to 425 degrees F. Line a rimmed baking sheet with aluminum foil and coat with cooking spray. (This will make cleanup a breeze.) Place the wings in a single layer on the foil and roast for 30 minutes; drain off any excess liquid.

✳ In a large bowl, combine remaining ingredients, except sesame seeds; mix well. Set aside ½ cup of this mixture for later. Add wings to the mixture in the bowl and toss until they're evenly coated, then return them to the baking sheet.

✳ Roast an additional 25 to 30 minutes or until the sauce begins to caramelize and the wings are crispy. Right before serving, toss the wings with the sauce you set aside. Sprinkle with sesame seeds and serve immediately.

Chef Tony's Tip: In my house I always keep a bottle or two of Thai sweet chili sauce on hand, just like I do ketchup and mustard. It's not too sweet, not too spicy, and adds just the right oomph to just about everything.

Amazing Appetizers

balsamic-kissed bruschetta

Serves 6-8

I have a confession. I have a brown thumb! I'm not much of a gardener, but growing up, my mom did keep a garden. Almost everyone in our neighborhood did. There were times when she'd have huge amounts of fresh parsley or basil (more than she knew what to do with), so she'd chop it and freeze it in ice cube trays so she could use it all year long. These days, whenever I chop fresh herbs, I always think of her. It's a sweet memory.

1 cup balsamic vinegar

½ cup light brown sugar

10 plum tomatoes, seeded and chopped

2 cloves garlic, finely chopped

⅓ cup olive oil

⅓ cup slivered fresh basil

1 teaspoon salt

1 teaspoon black pepper

1 loaf French bread, sliced diagonally into 1-inch-thick slices

Cooking spray

✸ In a small saucepan over high heat, bring balsamic vinegar to a boil. Stir in brown sugar, reduce heat to low, and simmer 12 to 15 minutes or until liquid is reduced and slightly thickened. Remove from heat and allow to cool slightly. Do not refrigerate this!

✸ In a large bowl, combine tomatoes, garlic, oil, basil, salt, and pepper; mix well.

✸ Right before serving, preheat broiler. Coat a baking sheet with cooking spray. Place bread slices on baking sheet and lightly spray tops with cooking spray. (Spraying the bread will make these crisp up while they cook.) Broil 2 to 3 minutes or until golden.

✸ Place bread slices on a serving platter, then spoon the tomato mixture over each slice of bread, and drizzle with balsamic glaze. Serve immediately.

Chef Tony's Tip: For parties, I like to serve the tomato mixture in a bowl with pita or bagel chips on the side.

come & get 'em cocktail meatballs

Serves 10-12

To make entertaining easy when the family comes over to watch a game or to help decorate the tree for the holidays, I just set out the slow cooker and a bunch of toothpicks, and let everyone help themselves to these amazing mini meatballs. They feature a crave-worthy cranberry-Asian flavor that makes them really popular!

1 (14-ounce) can whole berry cranberry sauce

⅓ cup hoisin sauce

⅓ cup ketchup

2 tablespoons rice vinegar

2 tablespoons soy sauce

1 teaspoon garlic powder

½ teaspoon ground ginger

2 pounds frozen mini meatballs (See Tip)

1 teaspoon sesame seeds (optional)

✳ In a 5-quart or larger slow cooker, combine cranberry sauce, hoisin sauce, ketchup, rice vinegar, soy sauce, garlic powder, and ginger; mix well. Stir in meatballs.

✳ Cover and cook on HIGH for 1-½ to 2 hours or on LOW for 2-½ to 3 hours or until heated through. Garnish with sesame seeds, if desired. (I always do!)

Chef Tony's Tip: I'm proud of my homemade meatballs, but every once in a while, I use the shortcut frozen ones to save on time.

mom's favorite zucchini fries

Serves 6-8

My mom used to love to go to this restaurant on Coney Island that served zucchini fries. It was one of her favorite snacks, so I learned how to make them myself and it turns out that they're pretty easy to make. They're a lower-carb and tasty alternative to traditional fries, and can be served as a side dish, snack, or appetizer. I hope you enjoy these as much as my family does!

3 large zucchini

½ teaspoon salt

⅛ teaspoon black pepper

¼ cup all-purpose flour

1 cup panko bread crumbs

½ teaspoon Italian seasoning

2 eggs

2 tablespoons milk

Cooking spray

✿ Preheat oven to 425 degrees F. Coat a baking sheet with cooking spray.

✿ Cut each zucchini lengthwise into ½-inch slices. Then cut each slice into ¼-inch "french fries" about 3 inches long. Place the zucchini in a medium bowl and sprinkle with salt and pepper; toss to coat evenly.

✿ Place flour in a shallow dish. Place bread crumbs and Italian seasoning in another shallow dish; mix well. In a third shallow dish, beat together the eggs and milk.

✿ Dip each zucchini strip in the flour, then dip into the egg mixture, and coat with the bread crumb mixture, before placing on the baking sheet.

✿ Spray the breaded zucchini with cooking spray. (Yes, spray the zucchini, not just the baking sheet. It helps them crisp up.) Bake 25 to 30 minutes or until golden. Serve immediately.

Chef Tony's Tip: When I make these for a crowd, I like to set out a few different dipping sauces, so that there's something for everybody. Feel free to experiment, but some of my favorite dippers are marinara, ranch, blue cheese dressing, and honey mustard.

Amazing Appetizers

bacon-wrapped sea scallops

Makes about 2 dozen

This was an appetizer at my favorite Chinese restaurant in Brooklyn, when I was a kid. An easy way to fancy up any party is to add these to your menu. Bacon-wrapped anything is going to be popular, but the combination of the scallops and water chestnuts takes these to a whole new level. Factor in the rumaki-style dipping sauce, and you've got yourself an appetizer that's sure to be the talk of your event. Trust me, I make this one all the time.

¾ pound bacon

1 (8-ounce) can sliced water chestnuts, drained

1 pound sea scallops, rinsed and patted dry

1 cup ketchup

⅓ cup packed light brown sugar

½ cup white vinegar

1 teaspoon Worcestershire sauce

✳ Cut bacon slices in half crosswise. Place a water chestnut on top of each scallop and wrap with a slice of bacon. Secure with a wooden toothpick and place on a rimmed baking sheet. (These can be made the day before and kept refrigerated until you're ready to bake them.)

✳ Before serving, preheat oven to 425 degrees F. Bake 15 to 18 minutes or until scallops are cooked through and bacon is crispy.

✳ While these bake, in a medium saucepan over medium heat, combine ketchup, brown sugar, vinegar, and Worcestershire sauce; mix well and simmer 5 to 7 minutes or until sugar is completely dissolved. Dip scallops in sauce and serve with remaining sauce.

cheesy mac & bacon bites

Makes 36

I used to make these a lot when I was in catering. Guests would make these disappear from the trays (along with the mini holdogs)! Now, I make them for all of my parties or anytime I have a movie night at home. The cheesy macaroni is amazing, and the little bits of bacon in every bite are just killer. I'm warning you – it isn't easy to have just one of these.

2 tablespoons butter

3 tablespoons all-purpose flour

1-½ cups milk

2 cups shredded extra-sharp cheddar cheese

1 teaspoon ground mustard

¼ teaspoon black pepper

8 ounces elbow macaroni, cooked and drained

½ cup crumbled cooked bacon

1 cup shredded mozzarella cheese

✽ Preheat oven to 350 degrees F. Coat 36 mini muffin tin cups with cooking spray.

✽ In a large saucepan over low heat, melt butter. Stir in flour and cook 1 minute or until golden. Gradually whisk in milk and cook until thickened, stirring constantly. Add cheddar cheese, ground mustard, and pepper; stir until cheese is melted.

✽ Remove from heat and stir in the cooked macaroni, bacon, and mozzarella cheese. Evenly spoon mixture into muffin tin cups.

✽ Bake 15 to 18 minutes or until heated through. Allow these to rest 4 to 5 minutes (to set up), before removing them from the muffin tin cups. (The easiest way to get them out is to run a knife around the edge of each cup.) Serve immediately.

Chef Tony's Tip: You can bake these ahead of time and just reheat them when you're ready to serve them. Also, I suggest putting a little extra shredded cheddar and some bacon bits on top to make them even better.

bubblin' hot
shrimp & artichoke dip

Serves 18-20

Crusty on top. Creamy on the inside. You can't go wrong with this baked shrimp and artichoke dip. It's so easy to throw together. If you're making it for a party, I suggest setting it out with some chunks of sourdough bread, and cut-up fresh veggies. It's a great way to showcase this mouthwatering dip which has become a staple in my house.

1 cup mayonnaise

1 (8-ounce) package cream cheese, softened

½ cup shredded mozzarella cheese

3 garlic cloves, minced

1 tablespoon Worcestershire sauce

1 tablespoon lemon juice

¼ teaspoon hot sauce

½ pound frozen cooked salad shrimp, thawed

½ cup coarsely chopped canned artichoke hearts

✳ Preheat oven to 350 degrees F. Coat a 1-quart baking dish with cooking spray.

✳ In a large bowl, combine mayonnaise, cream cheese, mozzarella cheese, garlic, Worcestershire sauce, lemon juice, and hot sauce; mix well. Stir in shrimp and artichokes; mix well. Spoon mixture into baking dish.

✳ Set baking dish on a rimmed baking sheet, just in case some of your dip bubbles over). Bake 25 to 30 minutes or until the center is bubblin' hot and the top is golden brown.

south-of-the-border bean dip

Serves 20-25

I'll be honest with you – I don't eat a whole lot of Mexican food. My family, on the other hand, they love it. And of course, I've made my fair share of Tex-Mex dishes in my catering days. This was one of my most popular dips. To this day, I still make it at home. The trick to eating this is to make sure you get a little bit of every layer when you dig in.

2 (9-ounce) cans bean dip

3 ripe avocados, mashed (about 1-½ cups)

½ cup mayonnaise

1 tablespoon lemon juice

1 (16-ounce) container sour cream

1 (1.25-ounce) package taco seasoning mix

1-½ cups (6 ounces) shredded cheddar cheese

4 scallions, finely chopped

1 tomato, diced

1 large bag of tortilla chips

✳ Spread bean dip in a 9-inch deep dish pie plate or on a large serving plate.

✳ In a large bowl, combine avocado, mayonnaise, and lemon juice; spread over bean dip. In another bowl, combine sour cream and taco seasoning; spread over avocado layer.

✳ Sprinkle with the cheese, the scallions, and the tomato. Cover and chill at least 4 hours before serving.

✳ Right before serving, place the chips on a rimmed baking sheet and warm in a 200-degree F oven for 10 minutes. Serve with the chilled dip.

Chef Tony's Tip: Since I love the taste of fresh herbs, I usually sprinkle freshly chopped cilantro on top right before serving.

"Soups are kind of a specialty of mine. I love experimenting by throwing different ingredients together and coming up with something really good."

soups, salads, and sandwiches

chicken pot pie all-star soup

Serves 4-6

My mom could turn leftovers into anything! She used to have a saying, which I've adapted into "musgo." Basically, if it's in the refrigerator it "must go." With that in mind, I came up with this all-star version of chicken pot pie in the form of a soup, using veggies I had left in my crisper (and in the freezer). It's so good, you'll want to fill your bathtub with it so you can dive in!

½ stick butter

½ cup chopped onion

1 stalk celery, sliced

½ pound fresh mushrooms, sliced

5 tablespoons all-purpose flour

4 cups chicken broth

½ teaspoon salt

⅛ teaspoon black pepper

2 cups frozen peas and carrots

1-½ cups diced cooked chicken

1 cup half-and-half

2 sprigs fresh thyme, stems removed

1 refrigerated rolled pie crust (from a 14.1-ounce box)

❋ Preheat oven to 425 degrees F.

❋ In a soup pot over medium heat, melt the butter. Add onion and celery and cook 5 minutes or until tender. Add mushrooms and cook 3 minutes, stirring occasionally. Add flour and cook 1 minute, stirring constantly. Stir in the broth, salt, pepper, peas and carrots, and chicken, and bring to a boil. Then reduce heat to low and simmer 10 minutes. Slowly stir in half-and-half and thyme, and simmer for 5 more minutes or until thickened.

❋ Meanwhile, unroll pie crust and, using a star cookie cutter, (see Tip), cut out dough and place on baking sheet. (The number of stars you'll end up with will vary based on the size of the cookie cutter you use.) Bake 5 to 8 minutes or until golden brown.

❋ Spoon soup into bowls and top each with star-shaped pie crust pieces. Serve immediately.

Chef Tony's Tip: If you don't have a star-shaped cookie cutter, you can just cut the dough into 2-inch squares and proceed as directed. You can also cut your pie crust into other fun shapes using whatever cookie cutters you have at home. (You might even want to use the other crust in the box to make extra because they're so good!)

slow cooker
sausage & bean soup

Serves 6-8

Between the sausage, the beans, and the greens, this one is a real favorite! I love sitting down to one of these hearty bowls. And although I don't use slow cookers very often, when I do, it's nice to end up with something tasty without having to break a sweat. It also allows me to spend some extra time with Vivian and our family, or have dinner waiting for me when I get home from QVC.

1 pound pork sausage, casings removed

4 cups chopped escarole

1 onion, chopped

2 stalks celery, chopped

2 (16-ounce) cans cannellini beans

4 cups beef broth

1 (28-ounce) can crushed tomatoes, undrained

1 teaspoon ground cumin

1 teaspoon salt

½ teaspoon black pepper

✳ In a large skillet over medium-high heat, brown sausage 6 to 8 minutes or until it's no longer pink, stirring to crumble. Drain any pan drippings.

✳ Place sausage in a 5-quart or larger slow cooker. Add remaining ingredients and stir well.

✳ Cover and cook on HIGH 5 hours or on LOW 8 to 9 hours or until the soup has thickened slightly and the escarole is tender.

Chef Tony's Tip: As for the pork sausage, you can use any you like — from sweet to spicy hot. I like one that's somewhere in the middle so I get a little kick, but the spiciness of the sausage doesn't overpower all of the other flavors.

restaurant-style french onion soup

Serves 6

Pull out the white tablecloth! Set out the good silverware! This soup tastes like something you would find on the menu of a really fancy restaurant. In it, you've got two different kinds of sweet-tasting onions swimming in a really flavorful beef broth that's topped with a crusty piece of bread and two melty cheeses. You'll feel like you're dining in a Parisian bistro – bon appetit!

3 tablespoons butter

2 medium red onions, thinly sliced

2 large sweet onions, thinly sliced

5 cups beef broth

1 cup apple cider

¼ teaspoon salt

½ teaspoon black pepper

½ cup grated Parmesan cheese

⅓ cup dry red wine

6 (1-inch) slices French bread, toasted

6 slices mozzarella cheese

6 slices Swiss or Gruyère cheese

✸ In a soup pot over medium heat, melt butter. Add the red and sweet onions and cook them for 20 to 25 minutes or until golden, stirring occasionally. (It takes time for the onions to get really caramelized, but it's worth the wait!)

✸ Add beef broth, cider, salt, and pepper; bring to a boil. Reduce heat to low, stir in the Parmesan cheese and wine, and cook 3 to 5 minutes or until the cheese is melted and the soup is heated through.

✸ Preheat oven to 450 degrees F. Place 6 oven-proof soup crocks on a rimmed baking sheet. Ladle soup evenly into crocks. Top each crock with a slice of bread, a slice of mozzarella cheese, and a slice of Swiss cheese.

✸ Place soup crocks in the oven for about 10 minutes until the cheese melts and the edges begin to get golden. Serve immediately.

Chef Tony's Tip: If you don't have oven-proof crocks, you can place the slices of bread on a baking sheet and top each piece with a slice of each cheese. Then, bake them in the oven for a couple of minutes. When the cheese has melted, place one on top of each bowl of soup and enjoy.

chillin'-out minestrone

Serves 8-10

No, I don't serve my minestrone chilled. I call this my "chillin'-out" soup, because I make it when I'm chillin' out at home. The beans and the barley make this one really hearty, so don't plan on doing a whole lot after finishing off a bowl. My suggestion? Pick out a good movie and get really cozy on the couch.

2 tablespoons olive oil

½ cup chopped onion

2 carrots, diced

1 stalk celery, diced

4 cloves garlic, minced

5 cups vegetable broth

1 (28-ounce) can crushed tomatoes

1 zucchini, cut into ½-inch chunks

2 cups frozen cut green beans

1 (15-ounce) can red kidney beans, drained

½ cup quick-cooking barley

½ teaspoon dried oregano

Parmesan cheese for sprinkling

✹ In a soup pot over medium-high heat, heat oil until hot; sauté onion, carrots, celery, and garlic for 4 to 5 minutes or until tender.

✹ Add broth, crushed tomatoes, zucchini, green beans, and kidney beans. Bring to a boil, reduce heat to low, and simmer for 10 minutes.

✹ Stir in barley and oregano, and cook an additional 15 minutes or until barley is tender. Spoon into bowls and sprinkle with Parmesan cheese.

Chef Tony's Tip: If you let this sit for a while or if you store some in the fridge overnight, you might need to add a little more broth to the soup before reheating it, since the barley tends to soak up all the goodness.

love-in-a-bowl chicken soup

Serves 6-7

No matter how your day is going, coming home to a bowl of this will make everything just a little bit better. This "love in a bowl" soup brings back childhood memories of Sarah, my Jewish nanny, and those times when she'd make chicken soup in big batches for our whole family. She'd make hers with what you'd consider "regular" chicken, but I like to use Cornish hens, since I think they give the broth a richer taste.

2 Cornish hens (1 to 1-½ pounds each)

10 cups cold water

3 carrots, cut into chunks

3 parsnips, cut into chunks

2 stalks celery, cut into chunks

1 onion, cut into chunks

1 tablespoon chopped fresh dill

1 tablespoon salt

1-½ teaspoons black pepper

½ (24-ounce) package frozen homestyle egg noodles

✳ In a soup pot over high heat, combine all of the ingredients except the noodles; bring to a boil. Reduce heat to low and simmer 2 to 2-1/2 hours or until the chicken is almost fall-apart tender.

✳ Meanwhile, in another pot, cook the noodles according to package directions.

✳ Using tongs, remove the hens from the soup and place on a rimmed baking sheet to cool slightly. Using kitchen shears, cut each hen in quarters. Place the cut-up pieces of the hens back in the pot, and simmer to keep warm.

✳ When ready to serve, distribute noodles evenly into bowls. Place a piece or two of chicken in each bowl and ladle soup over noodles.

Chef Tony's Tip: If you prefer to add matzo balls instead of noodles, here's how to make mine: In a medium bowl, combine 4 eggs, 1/2 cup melted shortening, 1/4 cup seltzer, and 1 teaspoon salt. Add 1 cup matzo meal (you can find this in the ethnic section of your grocery store) and stir until combined. Cover and chill 30 minutes. Wet hands slightly, then form mixture into 1-inch balls; drop into a pot of boiling water. Cover and simmer 20 minutes or until they float. Add to soup during the last 15 minutes of cooking.

Soups, Salads, and Sandwiches

creamy clam chowder

Serves 4-5

Growing up in Brooklyn, the ocean was just a stone's throw from my home. We took advantage of this and went clamming whenever we had the opportunity. And with all of those clams you can bet we all ate lots of clam chowder. However, instead of making it Manhattan-style (tomato base), we usually ate it the New England way (cream base). When clams weren't in season, canned ones did the trick – just like they do here.

1 tablespoon vegetable oil

½ cup chopped celery

¼ cup finely chopped onion

2 (10-ounce) cans whole baby clams, undrained

2 (8-ounce) bottles clam juice

1 large potato, peeled and diced

½ teaspoon dried thyme leaf

½ teaspoon salt

¼ teaspoon black pepper

3 tablespoons all-purpose flour

2 cups half-and-half, divided

1 tablespoon chopped fresh parsley

✳ In a soup pot over medium heat, heat oil until hot; sauté celery and onion 5 to 7 minutes or until tender. Add the canned clams (make sure you add the liquid from the can too), the clam juice, potato, thyme, salt, and pepper.

✳ Cover and bring to a boil. Cook 10 to 12 minutes or until potato is tender.

✳ In a small bowl, whisk flour and 1/2 cup half-and-half; slowly whisk into the soup. Add remaining 1-½ cups half-and-half and the parsley; cook 5 minutes or until thickened, stirring frequently.

Chef Tony's Tip: Make sure to pick up a bag of oyster crackers to go with this when you're at the grocery store. They're fun to eat with or without the soup!

the perfect chopped salad

Serves 5-6

I make this salad once or twice a week for myself, and it's on every menu at all of our get-togethers. I love a good chopped salad, and this one is more than good — it's perfect. One of the best things about it is that you can eat it with a spoon! For some reason, that just makes it even better for me. Replace your standard side salad with this one, and just watch how fast it disappears!

Vinaigrette Dressing

½ cup olive oil

1 tablespoon Dijon mustard

1 tablespoon chopped fresh parsley

1 teaspoon dried oregano

½ teaspoon garlic powder

½ teaspoon salt

¼ teaspoon black pepper

¼ cup red wine vinegar

1 cucumber, diced

1 cup cherry tomatoes, quartered

1 (14-ounce) can artichoke hearts, drained and chopped

2 stalks celery, chopped

1 (12-ounce) jar roasted red peppers, drained and chopped

6 pepperoncini, sliced

1 (4-ounce) can black olives, drained and sliced

½ cup crumbled feta cheese

✳ To make my homemade Vinaigrette Dressing, in a bowl, whisk together oil, mustard, parsley, oregano, garlic powder, salt, and pepper. Add vinegar and whisk until well blended. Set aside.

✳ In a large bowl, combine cucumber, tomatoes, artichoke hearts, celery, red peppers, pepperoncini, and olives. Pour dressing over vegetables and toss to coat evenly. Sprinkle with feta and serve.

Chef Tony's Tip: Don't be afraid to add more veggies to this one, or swap out something you don't like. The only rule is everything needs to be cut small, so you can still eat this with a spoon.

tasty turkey cobb salad

Serves 5-6

I make a lot of salads, and one of my favorite things to do is to mix and match different textures to make eating them a lot more exciting (especially for people who say they don't like salads). The Cobb salad is a great one to do this with, because it's got a lot going on – crispy bacon, creamy avocado, and soft blue cheese (just to name a few).

1 head iceberg lettuce

8 slices cooked thick-cut bacon, crumbled

3 hard-boiled eggs, cut into wedges

1 avocado, peeled, pitted, and diced

2 tomatoes, diced

1 (2.25-ounce) can sliced black olives, drained

¼ pound blue cheese, crumbled

2 (¼-inch-thick) slices deli turkey, diced (about ½ pound)

1 cup Thousand Island dressing

✸ Place the whole, uncut head of iceberg lettuce in a large bowl and cover it with ice water. Allow to sit 20 minutes (this will make it extra crisp). Drain the lettuce well and cut it into 2-inch chunks.

✸ Place the lettuce on a large platter. Arrange the remaining ingredients, except the dressing, in rows over the lettuce.

✸ Right before serving, you can drizzle the dressing all over the salad or you could serve it on the side and let everyone spoon it onto their own plates.

Chef Tony's Tip: To make your own Thousand Island dressing, simply mix together 2 cups mayo, 1/4 cup ketchup, and 1/2 cup pickle relish that you've drained really well. Serve immediately and store any extra in the fridge in a covered container for up to 2 weeks.

shortcut caesar salad

Serves 4-5

When I worked in the restaurant business, I remember making lots of Caesar salads. Back then, we did it the old school way – starting each batch by mashing the garlic and anchovies in a big wooden bowl. Nowadays, when I'm craving a Caesar salad, I don't go through all that trouble. This shortcut version comes together in no time and the results are second to none.

Caesar Dressing

1 cup mayonnaise

½ cup milk

2 tablespoons fresh lemon juice

½ cup grated Parmesan cheese

2 cloves garlic, minced

½ teaspoon salt

½ teaspoon black pepper

1 tablespoon anchovy paste (optional)

1 head romaine lettuce, cut into bite-sized pieces

2 cups croutons

1 tablespoon grated Parmesan cheese

❋ To make Caesar Dressing, in a medium bowl, combine mayonnaise, milk, lemon juice, ½ cup Parmesan cheese, the garlic, salt, pepper, and anchovy paste, if desired. Whisk until smooth and creamy; set aside.

❋ In a large bowl, combine romaine and croutons. Add some of the dressing; toss to coat well. If needed, add more dressing or refrigerate for a later use.

❋ Sprinkle with remaining 1 tablespoon Parmesan cheese. Serve immediately.

Chef Tony's Tip: Before you roll your eyes at the anchovy paste, make sure you give it a try! If you don't see it at your local grocery store, just ask — it's there somewhere. It adds a welcoming, salty touch to the salad without the "not so familiar" texture that's usually associated with whole anchovies.

shrimp salad stuffed tomatoes

Makes 2

Yeah, baby! Something I look forward to every summer is getting my hands on really fresh, locally grown tomatoes, and stuffing them with all of my favorite salads. Sometimes it's shrimp salad (like here), but other times I go with chicken, tuna, or even my perfect chopped salad (page 56). One of the reasons why I like these so much is that they LOOK great (check it out for yourself!), but the main reason is...well, there's nothing like a sun-ripened tomato!

Shrimp Salad

1 cup cooked salad shrimp

2 tablespoons mayonnaise

¼ cup sliced celery

¼ teaspoon seafood seasoning

¼ teaspoon celery salt

⅛ teaspoon black pepper

½ teaspoon fresh lemon juice

2 large tomatoes

4 Boston Bibb lettuce leaves

1 tablespoon chopped chives

4 lemon wedges

✳ To make Shrimp Salad, in a medium bowl, combine shrimp, mayonnaise, celery, seafood seasoning, celery salt, pepper, and lemon juice; mix well. (I like to use the mayo sparingly here, but if you like yours more "dressed up," go ahead and add a bit more.)

✳ With a paring knife, cut out the center of the tomatoes, creating a bowl. (Check out the picture if you need help!)

✳ Place a couple of lettuce leaves on each plate and top each with a tomato. Spoon the shrimp salad evenly into tomatoes, sprinkle with chives, and serve with lemon wedges.

Chef Tony's Tip: You can use the part of the tomato that you scooped out to make tomato sauce. Waste not, want not!

shake-it-up lemon vinaigrette

Makes ¾ cup

For someone who loves salads as much as I do, it's a necessity to know how to throw together an easy, basic vinaigrette that you can drizzle over your favorite greens. This is one that's a staple in my house. You can "shake it up" in just about any old jar you have lying around the house. It'll add a fresh, bright flavor to any of your salads!

2 tablespoons red or white wine vinegar

1 teaspoon Italian seasoning

1 clove garlic, minced

¼ teaspoon ground mustard

½ teaspoon kosher salt

¼ teaspoon black pepper

½ cup olive oil

3 tablespoons fresh lemon juice

✳ In a 1 cup or larger glass jar with a tight-fitting lid, combine the vinegar, Italian seasoning, garlic, ground mustard, salt, pepper, oil, and lemon juice. Make sure the top is on tight (if you want to avoid a mess!) and shake it really well. (Shake, shake, shake. Shake, shake, shake. Shake your dressing. Shake your dressing. I know, I'm old school!)

✳ Serve immediately or store in the refrigerator until ready to use.

Chef Tony's Tip: This may be my basic recipe, but don't be scared to make it your own. For example, you can use fresh herbs, like basil and oregano, if you have them on hand, in place of the Italian seasoning. And if you do, make sure you add them in healthy tablespoons, rather than teaspoons, since you typically need 1 tablespoon of fresh herbs for every 1 teaspoon of dried.

Soups, Salads, and Sandwiches

mandarin beet salad with poppy dressing

Serves 2-3

I don't know who the first person was that decided to put beets and oranges together, but I'm really glad they did. This salad is colorful and a great "gourmet" choice if you're trying to impress someone. The earthy flavors of the beets complement the citrusy ones of the oranges, while the crumbled goat cheese adds a creamy and tangy taste that pairs perfectly with the sweet and zesty dressing.

Poppy Dressing

¼ cup Italian dressing

2 tablespoons sugar

½ teaspoon poppy seeds

¼ cup pine nuts

2 tablespoons maple syrup

4 cups mixed baby salad greens

1 (8.25-ounce) can sliced beets, drained and cut in half

½ cup mandarin oranges, drained

2 tablespoons crumbled goat cheese

✳ To make Poppy Dressing, in a small bowl, whisk together Italian dressing, sugar, and poppy seeds until sugar is dissolved; set aside.

✳ In a small skillet over medium heat, toast pine nuts 3 to 4 minutes or until they start to brown, stirring occasionally. (Keep an eye on them, as once they start toasting, they brown quickly). Add the syrup and stir to coat evenly; let cool.

✳ Place greens in a shallow bowl. Top with beets, mandarin oranges, maple-glazed pine nuts, and goat cheese. Drizzle with the dressing and serve.

Chef Tony's Tip: When fresh beets (red or golden ones) are available, I use them instead of the canned ones. To prepare them, I trim off the ends, coat them with olive oil, and season them with a little salt and pepper. Then I roast them until they're tender, and peel and cut them before putting them into my salad.

Soups, Salads, and Sandwiches

mom's special patty melts

Makes 4

These are really special to me because they were one of my mom's favorites. My mom was the youngest of 16 children, and learned early on how to help cook for the family. So it didn't take long for her to become a "gourmet." Out of all of the great things she made, believe it or not, patty melts were her favorite. While she's no longer with us today, every year on her birthday, we celebrate her love of food by making these. Love you mom!

5 tablespoons butter, divided

1 large onion, thinly sliced

1-½ pounds ground beef

¼ cup plus 1 teaspoon steak sauce, divided

¼ teaspoon salt

¼ teaspoon black pepper

8 slices rye bread

8 slices Swiss cheese

❋ In a large skillet over medium-high heat, melt 1 tablespoon butter; sauté onion 6 to 8 minutes or until it starts to brown. Remove to a bowl and cover.

❋ In a large bowl, combine ground beef and 1 teaspoon steak sauce. Form the beef into 4 oval patties; sprinkle with salt and pepper. (Don't make your patties too thick; you want them about the size of the bread.)

❋ Place the patties in the same skillet that you cooked the onions in, and over medium heat, cook 5 to 7 minutes per side or until patties are medium or to desired doneness beyond that. Remove from skillet and keep warm.

❋ Spread remaining butter over one side of each slice of bread. After carefully wiping the skillet clean (careful, it may still be hot!), place 2 slices of bread, buttered-side down, in the skillet over medium heat. Top each with a slice of cheese, then with a cooked patty, a quarter of the cooked onions, and 1 tablespoon of the steak sauce. Top with another slice of cheese and finally top them off with another slice of bread (buttered-side up).

❋ Cook until the bottom piece of bread is golden, then flip it over. When the bottom piece is golden and the cheese is melted, it's done. Transfer to a serving platter and cover to keep warm. Repeat with remaining ingredients. Serve immediately.

Chef Tony's Tip: You can always make these taste more like the ones they serve in New York delis by replacing the steak sauce that's schmeared on the bread (not what's in the burger) with Russian dressing.

roast beef italian heroes

Makes 2

There's nothing like freshly cooked roast beef. Back in the day, Brooklyn was full of luncheonettes that served it. There was one every 2 to 3 blocks. One stands out in my memory – I remember walking in and seeing what looked like a side of beef on a rotisserie behind the counter. When I ordered a hero, they sliced it fresh from that big piece. Then they dipped it in some broth and piled it on a crusty roll, before topping it with cheese. I don't think I'll ever forget how good that was.

1 cup beef broth

½ teaspoon onion powder

¼ teaspoon black pepper

½ pound thinly sliced deli roast beef

2 hoagie rolls, cut in half lengthwise

4 slices provolone cheese

½ cup giardiniera mix, coarsely chopped

2 tablespoons banana pepper rings

❈ Preheat broiler.

❈ In a small skillet over medium-high heat, bring broth, onion powder, and black pepper to a boil. Using tongs, dip the roast beef slices into the broth for 10 seconds, then place them on the bottom half of hoagie rolls, dividing evenly. (Don't worry about draining the meat, since the broth is what makes this sandwich extra flavorful.) Top each with 2 slices of cheese and place under the broiler for 2 minutes or until cheese is melted.

❈ Remove sandwiches from broiler. Evenly divide the chopped giardiniera mix and banana pepper rings between the sandwiches. Place the tops of the rolls back on and serve with a side of beef broth for drizzling or dunking along the way.

Chef Tony's Tip: If you're not familiar with giardiniera, it's simply an assortment of pickled cauliflower, carrots, peppers and what-not. You can find this at the grocery store, right next to all of the pickles. It's a must-have in my fridge

Soups, Salads, and Sandwiches

thanksgiving dinner deli wrap

Makes 4

Vivian, my beautiful fiancé, is a big fan of this one! What she likes about this (and so does everyone else in our family) is that it allows her to enjoy the comforting taste of Thanksgiving all year long. These are easy to make, so you can satisfy your cravings, without all the work. Every bite delivers just the right amount of Thanksgiving goodness!

½ cup mayonnaise

4 (10-inch) flour tortillas

4 leaves leaf lettuce

¾ pound thinly sliced deli turkey

2 cups prepared stuffing, warmed (see Tip)

½ cup whole berry cranberry sauce (see Tip)

❋ Spread mayonnaise evenly on tortillas. Top each with a lettuce leaf and ¼ of the turkey slices. Spoon stuffing evenly onto center and top each, evenly, with the cranberry sauce.

❋ Fold bottom of tortilla over the filling, then tuck both sides in over it, in an envelope style. Roll it up and place each one seam-side down on a platter.

❋ Right before serving, place the wraps in a large skillet over medium heat for about 5 minutes per side. Heat until the tortilla is golden and the filling is slightly warmed through. Cut each in half diagonally, and serve.

Chef Tony's Tip: For the stuffing, I like to use a boxed stuffing mix — that way I can just make the amount that I need. If you prefer, you can use jellied cranberry sauce instead of whole berry.

peanut butter & jelly monte cristo

Makes 4

My two favorite sandwiches in the world are a basic PB&J (made with strawberry jam) and a Monte Cristo. One day, curiosity got the best of me, and I decided to try and mash the two together. Little did I know, I was about to create one of the best sandwiches ever. It took just one bite (when the warm peanut butter and jelly oozed out between the egg-battered, pan-fried bread) to realize that this was going to be a new favorite.

4 eggs

⅓ cup milk

½ teaspoon vanilla extract

½ cup peanut butter

½ cup strawberry jam

8 slices home-style bread

¾ cup vegetable oil

Powdered sugar for sprinkling

✳ In a shallow dish, whisk eggs, milk, and vanilla until well combined.

✳ Spread the peanut butter and jam evenly on 4 slices of bread. Top with the remaining 4 slices of bread, creating 4 sandwiches.

✳ In a medium skillet over medium heat, heat oil until hot. Dip one sandwich in the egg mixture, turning it over until it's coated completely. Place it in the skillet and cook 1 to 1-½ minutes on each side or until bread is golden. Remove to a paper towel-lined platter. Repeat with remaining sandwiches. Sprinkle with powdered sugar and serve.

Chef Tony's Tip: Make this recipe your own by changing up the bread. I've made this on challah (egg bread) and it's just as amazing. As for the jam, feel free to use your personal favorite, like I did.

There's a saying that's perfect for our family..."Some people eat to live, but we live to eat!"

plenty of poultry

sheet pan greek chicken supper

Serves 4-6

You can always make a home-cooked meal, even when you're really busy. This one only takes about 10 minutes to prep before it goes into the oven. You can finish getting things done while it's roasting, which is really great for those busy weeknights. I don't know about you, but just looking at this photo gets my taste buds excited!

½ cup olive oil

3 tablespoons lemon juice

4 cloves garlic, slivered

1 tablespoon chopped fresh parsley

1 teaspoon dried oregano

1 teaspoon salt

½ teaspoon black pepper

8 red potatoes, cut in half

1 (4-to 5-pound) whole chicken, cut into quarters

1-½ cups cherry tomatoes

¼ cup pitted Kalamata olives

✳ Preheat oven to 350 degrees F.

✳ In a large bowl, combine oil, lemon juice, garlic, parsley, oregano, salt, and pepper; mix well. Add the potatoes and toss until evenly coated. Place the potatoes on a large rimmed baking sheet. Make sure you keep any of the oil mixture that's left in the bowl; don't pour it onto the tray.

✳ Place the chicken pieces, one piece at a time, into the remaining oil mixture, and toss to coat. Arrange the chicken on the baking sheet, nestling the pieces between the potatoes.

✳ Roast 45 minutes, then add the tomatoes around the chicken, and continue to cook for 15 more minutes or until no pink remains and the skin is browned and crispy. Sprinkle with olives and serve.

Chef Tony's Tip: Add a fresh look by garnishing with some sprigs of fresh oregano. It adds an amazing aroma too!

anytime bbq chicken

Serves 3-4

Rain or shine, you'll be able to enjoy my BBQ chicken anytime – that's because it's cooked in the oven. These chicken drumsticks are covered in a flavorful homemade barbecue sauce that you're going to be licking off of your fingers (at least I do...). Make a double batch and invite the neighbors over. They'll be so glad you did!

5 tablespoons all-purpose flour, divided

2 teaspoons salt, divided

8 chicken drumsticks

1/3 cup vegetable oil

1/2 onion, chopped

1/2 green bell pepper, chopped

2 stalks celery, chopped

1 cup ketchup

1 cup cola

2 tablespoons Worcestershire sauce

1/2 teaspoon dried basil

2 teaspoons chili powder

1/8 teaspoon black pepper

✳ Preheat oven to 350 degrees F. Coat a 9- x 13-inch baking dish with cooking spray.

✳ In a shallow dish or pie plate, combine 2 tablespoons flour and 1 teaspoon salt. Rinse the chicken and pat it dry. Coat the chicken evenly with the flour mixture and set aside.

✳ In a large skillet over medium heat, heat oil until hot. Brown chicken 5 to 8 minutes or until the skin is golden and crisp. Place in the baking dish.

✳ In a large bowl, combine the remaining ingredients, including the 3 tablespoons remaining flour and the 1 teaspoon remaining salt; mix well. Spoon the sauce evenly over the chicken. Cover tightly with aluminum foil and roast 50 minutes. Uncover, baste, and cook an additional 5 minutes or until no pink remains.

Chef Tony's Tip: I like to chop all of the veggies for the sauce with my mini food chopper, since I can just toss everything in and have it done in seconds. Also, I've been known to substitute wings for the drumsticks from time to time.

slow cooker dunkin' chicken

Serves 4-5

I like to serve this chicken dish in a bowl, because it's got a flavor-packed broth. That means you've got to make sure you serve it with a loaf of crusty bread too. You can use it to dunk into the broth – making sure not to leave a single drop of goodness behind. I've found that this dish is really good for bringing the family together.

4 tablespoons olive oil, divided

1 (3-pound) chicken, cut into 8 pieces

1-½ cups sliced cremini mushrooms

1 onion, diced

2 cloves garlic, minced

1 cup chicken broth

1 (6-ounce) can tomato paste

⅓ cup dry red wine

2 teaspoons sugar

1 teaspoon dried oregano

½ teaspoon salt

¼ teaspoon black pepper

2 tablespoons slivered fresh basil

✸ In a large heavy skillet over medium heat, heat 2 tablespoons oil until hot. Brown the chicken pieces in batches. It should take about 3 to 5 minutes per side. Once browned, remove to a baking sheet and set aside. Add additional oil as needed.

✸ In a 6-quart or larger slow cooker, combine mushrooms, onion, and garlic. Place the browned chicken on top of the vegetable mixture. In a bowl, combine chicken broth, tomato paste, wine, sugar, oregano, salt, and pepper; pour over chicken.

✸ Cover and cook on LOW 7 to 8 hours or on HIGH 3 to 4 hours or until chicken is cooked through and no pink remains. Before serving, garnish with basil.

pretzel chicken with cheese sauce

Serves 4

Pretzels and cheese are two of my favorite snack foods. I used them both to come up with this chicken dish that's second to none. Now I can enjoy my favorite snacks at dinnertime too. I can't wait for you guys to tell me what you like best about this one! Will it be the crunchy pretzel coating, the Dijon mustard kick, or the cheesy topping? If you're like me, you won't be able to decide!

2 cups crushed salted pretzels

2 eggs

¼ cup Dijon mustard

¼ cup all-purpose flour

4 boneless, skinless chicken breasts, lightly pounded to ½-inch thickness

½ teaspoon onion powder

½ teaspoon salt

½ teaspoon black pepper

½ cup vegetable oil

½ cup cheese sauce, warmed (see Tip)

❂ Place crushed pretzels in a shallow dish or pie plate. In another shallow dish, whisk eggs and mustard. Place flour in a third shallow dish.

❂ Season both sides of each chicken breast with onion powder, salt, and pepper. Dip each breast in the flour, then the egg mixture, then the crushed pretzels. To ensure that you get an even crust, make sure to press the crushed pretzels firmly onto the chicken.

❂ In a large skillet over medium-low heat, heat oil until hot. Pan fry the chicken for 5 to 6 minutes per side or until no pink remains. You may need to do this in batches depending on the size of the chicken and your skillet.

❂ Drizzle chicken with cheese sauce and serve.

Chef Tony's Tip: You can make your own cheese sauce (like I do, on occasion) or, if you're making this as a quick, weeknight meal, you can just warm up a jarred cheese sauce, like cheez Whiz®. It does the trick and is a whole lot easier.

chicken divan casserole

Serves 5-6

This is the ultimate comfort food. (Well, except for my homemade lasagna.) I love how everything bakes together, and that with each forkful, you get the creaminess of the sauce, the heartiness of the chicken, and the fluffiness of the biscuits. Here's a trick for making sure nothing is left behind — use the last few biscuit pieces to sop up any remaining gravy!

1 (10-¾-ounce) can cream of chicken soup

1 cup sour cream

2 cups shredded cheddar cheese, divided

¾ teaspoon salt

½ teaspoon black pepper

3 cups diced cooked chicken

2 cups frozen chopped broccoli, thawed

¼ cup crumbled cooked bacon

1 (16.3-ounce) can refrigerated biscuits, each biscuit cut into thirds

✳ Preheat oven to 375 degrees F. Coat a 9- x 13-inch baking dish with cooking spray.

✳ In a large bowl, mix together soup, sour cream, 1-½ cups cheese, the salt, and pepper until well combined. Stir in chicken, broccoli, and bacon. Fold in the cut-up biscuits, making sure they're evenly coated.

✳ Spoon the mixture into the baking dish. Sprinkle with remaining ½ cup cheese. Bake 30 to 35 minutes or until the biscuits are golden brown and the center is hot.

my signature chicken parmesan

Serves 4

This is my signature chicken Parmesan. I serve it with spaghetti, in a sandwich, and even on top of sautéed greens. What makes it so good is just how flavorful it is. To get the most out of your dry spices (like the Italian seasoning in this), place them in the palm of your hand and rub your fingers over them, crushing them. This helps release some of the oils left in the seasonings and adds even more flavor.

¼ cup plus 1 tablespoon olive oil

1 small onion, finely chopped

2 cloves garlic, minced

1 (26-ounce) jar spaghetti sauce

2 tablespoons Italian seasoning, divided

1 cup plain bread crumbs

2 tablespoons Parmesan cheese

1-½ teaspoons garlic powder

2 eggs

1 tablespoon water

4 boneless, skinless chicken breasts, flattened to a ¼-inch thickness

Salt and black pepper for sprinkling

1 tablespoon butter

1 cup shredded mozzarella cheese

✺ Preheat oven to 350 degrees F. Coat a baking sheet with cooking spray. In a medium saucepan over medium heat, heat 1 tablespoon olive oil until hot. Sauté onion and garlic until golden, stirring occasionally. Add spaghetti sauce and 1 tablespoon Italian seasoning; simmer until ready to use. (By this point the kitchen will smell amazing.)

✺ In a shallow dish or pie plate, combine bread crumbs, the remaining 1 tablespoon Italian seasoning, Parmesan cheese, and garlic powder. In another shallow dish, whisk eggs and water. Evenly sprinkle both sides of chicken with salt and pepper.

✺ In a large skillet over medium-high heat, heat remaining ¼ cup of oil with the butter until hot. Dip the chicken in the egg mixture, then into the bread crumb mixture, pressing firmly, until well coated. Sauté chicken 5 to 6 minutes or until no pink remains and chicken is golden brown, turning halfway through.

✺ Remove cooked chicken to a baking sheet; repeat with remaining chicken. Evenly spoon sauce over chicken, then sprinkle with mozzarella cheese. Bake 5 to 7 minutes or until cheese is melted and starts to brown.

Chef Tony's Tip: This recipe is great as it is, but when time permits, I like to soak my cutlets in chicken broth in the fridge for 30 minutes before seasoning and cooking. This makes them extra moist.

bacon-wrapped chicken cordon bleu

Serves 4

This is one of my all-time favorite meals. Everyone should make chicken cordon bleu at least once in their life. It's a classic that can easily be made at home on a busy weeknight or for a dinner party with friends. Since I'm such a big fan of bacon, I like to add a whole new layer of flavor by wrapping each chicken breast with it. Serve it with a green veggie, like my Lemony Roasted Broccoli (page 160), and you're done!

4 boneless, skinless chicken breasts (1 to 1-¼ pounds)

¼ teaspoon salt

⅛ teaspoon black pepper

4 slices Swiss cheese

4 slices thinly-sliced deli ham

8 slices bacon (see Tip)

❈ Preheat oven to 350 degrees F. Coat a rimmed baking sheet with cooking spray.

❈ Between 2 pieces of wax paper, gently pound chicken to ¼-inch thickness with a mallet or rolling pin.

❈ Evenly sprinkle each piece of chicken with salt and pepper. Place 1 cheese slice and 1 ham slice on top of each chicken breast. Roll each breast jelly roll-style. Wrap each roll with 2 slices of bacon, and secure with a toothpick. Place on baking sheet seam-side down.

❈ Bake for 25 to 30 minutes or until chicken is no longer pink in center and bacon is crispy. Remove toothpicks before serving.

Chef Tony's Tip: Regular varieties of Swiss cheese and deli-style ham tend to be naturally salty, so if you'd rather not add the extra salt that's fine. Also, if you like your bacon really crispy, like I do, I recommend par-baking it on a rimmed baking sheet for 10 minutes, in a 400-degree oven. Let it cool slightly before wrapping it around the chicken.

even better bourbon chicken

Serves 5-6

Whenever I go to the mall, I make sure my visit includes a walk through the food court. That's the only way to see what's new, and also to fuel up on samples. No matter what mall I go to, there's always someone passing out pieces of bourbon chicken on toothpicks. Since these samples are popular, I decided to recreate this dish at home. I think my version is even better, but I'll leave it to you to be the judge.

2 pounds boneless, skinless chicken breasts, cut into 2-inch pieces

2 tablespoons cornstarch

1 teaspoon garlic powder

¼ teaspoon cayenne pepper (optional)

½ teaspoon salt

¼ cup canola oil

1 cup jalapeño pepper jelly

1 tablespoon soy sauce

2 tablespoons bourbon

✳ In a medium bowl, combine chicken, cornstarch, garlic powder, cayenne pepper, if desired, and salt; toss to coat well.

✳ In a large skillet over high heat, heat oil until hot. Add chicken, in batches, and cook for 6 to 8 minutes or until golden and no pink remains, stirring frequently.

✳ In a large saucepan over medium heat, bring jelly, soy sauce, and bourbon to a boil. Let simmer 2 to 3 minutes or until jelly has melted, stirring constantly. Add chicken and toss to coat. Serve hot.

Chef Tony's Tip: I often serve this over some basmati rice so it can soak up all the saucy goodness.

cheesy ranch chicken bake

Serves 4-5

Truth be told, I don't like ranch dressing, but my family does, and I know that many of my fellow foodies do too. So, I came up with this recipe just for you guys. It's an all-in-one, slow cooker feast that's got cheesy potatoes, bacon, and chicken, all smothered in creamy ranch dressing. I hope your family enjoys this one as much as mine does!

1 (32-ounce) package frozen potato tots

2 cups shredded cheddar cheese

1 cup shredded Monterey pepper jack cheese

1 (2.8-ounce) package cooked bacon pieces

1 (1-ounce) package ranch dressing mix

¼ teaspoon salt

¼ teaspoon black pepper

4 boneless, skinless chicken breasts, cut into 2-inch pieces

¾ cup milk

✲ Coat the bottom of a 6-quart slow cooker with cooking spray (so that the potato tots don't stick to it.)Then place half of the potato tots in the slow cooker.

✲ In a medium bowl, combine both of the cheeses; mix well. Sprinkle half of the cheese over the potato tots. Then sprinkle half of the bacon over the cheese.

✲ In a shallow dish, mix the ranch dressing mix with salt and pepper. Coat the chicken in the ranch mixture and place over the bacon pieces in the slow cooker. Sprinkle any of the remaining ranch mixture over the chicken. Top with the remaining potato tots, cheese, and bacon. Drizzle the milk over top.

✲ Cover and cook on LOW 6 to 8 hours or until no pink remains in the chicken and the cheese is ooey-gooey. Serve immediately.

crispy chicken fingers with garlic parm sauce

Serves 3-4

Chicken tenders are a must-have for kids. I couldn't even begin to tell you how many times I've made them for my kids and grandkids. With this recipe, you can make perfectly crispy, kid-approved tenders with the best dipping sauce on the planet. And just because these are kid-approved doesn't mean they aren't good for adults too. Hey, I like to tell myself that sometimes I'm just a really big kid!

1-¼ cups all-purpose flour

½ teaspoon salt

½ teaspoon garlic powder

½ teaspoon cayenne pepper (optional)

½ teaspoon black pepper

½ cup buttermilk

1 pound chicken tenders

1 cup vegetable shortening

Garlic Parm Sauce

4 tablespoons butter, divided

1-½ teaspoons minced garlic

½ cup heavy cream

½ cup grated Parmesan cheese

❊ In a shallow dish, combine flour, salt, garlic powder, cayenne pepper, if desired, and black pepper; mix well. Place buttermilk in another shallow dish. Dip the chicken tenders in the flour mixture, coating completely. Then dip the tenders in the buttermilk, and back in the flour mixture, coating completely.

❊ In a deep skillet over medium-low heat, heat shortening until hot, but not smoking (about 325 degrees F). Carefully add the chicken in batches, and fry 4 to 5 minutes per side or until golden and no pink remains. Drain on a paper towel-lined platter.

❊ Meanwhile, to make the Garlic Parm Sauce, in a saucepan over medium heat, melt 1 tablespoon butter; add garlic and sauté for 1 minute or until tender. Slowly stir in the cream and Parmesan cheese; reduce heat to low and simmer 3 to 4 minutes or until it thickens. (Do not boil.) Whisk in the remaining 3 tablespoons butter until melted.

❊ Spoon the sauce over the chicken or serve it on the side. Serve immediately.

Chef Tony's Tip: If you want to make these ahead of time, you can rewarm them on a baking sheet, in an oven that's been preheated to 300 degrees, for about 10 minutes.

kickin' chicken & kielbasa stew

Serves 4-6

When you've got a big family like I do, you learn to come up with meals that are easy to throw together and fill everyone up. I wish that I could tell you that every day I make a from-scratch pasta dish or that I have time to spend hours in the kitchen, but I'd be lying. Like everyone else, I rely on shortcuts like frozen veggies from time to time. They deliver the same great flavor, but help save prep time.

1 tablespoon vegetable oil

1 pound boneless, skinless chicken breasts, cut into ½-inch pieces

½ cup chopped onion

2 cloves garlic, minced

½ pound smoked kielbasa, sliced

1 (15.5-ounce) can Great Northern beans, undrained

1 (14.5-ounce) can diced tomatoes, undrained

2 cups frozen Italian green beans

1 cup frozen sliced carrots

1 teaspoon dried oregano

½ teaspoon salt

½ teaspoon black pepper

✳ In a soup pot over medium heat, heat oil until hot. Sauté chicken and onion for 5 to 7 minutes or until chicken is no longer pink. Add garlic and cook for 1 minute. Add remaining ingredients and bring to a boil.

✳ Reduce heat to low and simmer for 40 to 45 minutes or until slightly thickened, stirring occasionally. Serve piping hot.

stuffed & glazed cornish hens

Serves 2

Sharing is really important to me. It was something that was taught to me at a young age. When I had kids of my own, I made sure that they became "sharers" too, especially when il came to food. However, there's one time when I don't follow that rule, and it's when I'm serving Cornish hens. Cornish hens are just the right size for one person, so when I make them, everyone gets their very own.

1-½ cups apricot nectar, divided

2 tablespoons butter

1-½ cups stuffing mix

2 tablespoons chopped almonds

2 Cornish hens
(about 1 to 1-½ pounds each)

1 teaspoon poultry seasoning

½ teaspoon salt

1 tablespoon vegetable oil

✳ Preheat oven to 350 degrees F. Coat a roasting pan with cooking spray.

✳ In a medium saucepan over medium heat, combine ¾ cup nectar and the butter; bring to a boil. Remove from heat. Stir in the stuffing mix and almonds, cover, and allow to sit 5 minutes; set aside.

✳ Prepare the hens like you would if you were cleaning a chicken. Then rinse them in cold water and pat them dry with paper towels. Using a soup spoon, stuff each hen with the stuffing mixture, dividing evenly. (If there's a little extra stuffing left, put it in a ramekin, and bake it for the last 30 minutes of the hens' cooking time.)

✳ In a small bowl, combine the poultry seasoning, salt, and oil and completely rub each hen with the mixture. Place the remaining ¾ cup of the nectar in the roasting pan and add the hens.

✳ Roast for 30 minutes, then baste with the nectar, and continue roasting an additional 30 minutes or until the juices run clear and the skin is golden brown. Serve with pan drippings.

Chef Tony's Tip: If you want to prep these ahead of time, make sure you let the stuffing cool completely before placing it in the hens. Then place the hens in the refrigerator until you're ready to roast them.

easy baked turkey tetrazzini

Serves 4-6

Nothing says "come and get it!" like a steamy hot casserole that's right out of the oven. As you know, we eat a lot of spaghetti in my family, and yes, a lot of times we eat it the traditional way – with red sauce and meatballs. But sometimes, I mix things up and get creative with the pasta. That's when I whip up dishes like this one. This spaghetti casserole is hearty, comforting, and weeknight easy.

8 ounces spaghetti

1 stick butter, divided

8 ounces mushrooms, sliced

¼ cup all-purpose flour

2 cups chicken broth

½ cup white wine

1 cup milk

1-½ pounds raw turkey breast, cut into ½-inch pieces

Salt and pepper for seasoning

1 cup frozen peas

¾ cup grated Parmesan cheese, divided

¼ cup plain bread crumbs

✹ Preheat oven to 375 degrees F. Coat a 3-quart casserole dish with cooking spray. Cook the spaghetti according to the package directions. (Make sure you don't overcook it, since it will cook again in the casserole.)

✹ Meanwhile, in a soup pot over medium heat, melt 6 tablespoons butter; add mushrooms and cook for 4 to 5 minutes or until tender. Stir in flour and cook for 1 minute. Slowly stir in broth, wine, and milk and bring just to a boil. Reduce heat to low, and simmer for 5 minutes or until slightly thickened.

✹ Season turkey with salt and pepper. In a skillet, melt 1 tablespoon of butter and sauté the turkey until cooked through and golden. Add turkey to soup pot along with cooked spaghetti, peas, and ½ cup Parmesan cheese; mix well. Spoon into the casserole dish.

✹ In a small microwave-safe bowl, melt remaining 2 tablespoons butter in the microwave; add bread crumbs and remaining ¼ cup Parmesan cheese; mix well. Sprinkle evenly over the casserole.

✹ Bake for 35 to 40 minutes or until the center is heated through and the casserole is golden on top. Serve piping hot.

garlic & herb turkey burgers

Makes 4

When you're craving burgers, but want to keep things light, I suggest you make these turkey burgers. For anyone who thinks that turkey burgers tend to be dry - you're going to be in for a real surprise with this recipe. These are so juicy and packed with flavor, you'll be craving them even when you aren't interested in lighter alternatives.

1-½ pounds ground turkey breast

3 tablespoons garlic and herb cheese spread, plus extra for topping

⅓ cup Italian bread crumbs

1 tablespoon chopped fresh parsley

1 tablespoon chopped fresh chives

1 teaspoon salt

½ teaspoon black pepper

4 pretzel buns, cut in half

✻ In a large bowl, combine ground turkey, 3 tablespoons cheese spread, bread crumbs, parsley, chives, salt, and pepper; mix well. Form the mixture into 4 patties.

✻ Coat a large skillet or griddle with cooking spray. Over medium heat, cook the patties 8 to 10 minutes or until no pink remains, turning halfway through cooking.

✻ Serve on buns and top each with a dollop of garlic and herb cheese spread.

Chef Tony's Tip: Don't forget the toppings! I like to serve these with lettuce, tomatoes, onions, and fresh herbs.

"I never feel more blessed than when I'm sharing a meal with my family or friends. It's something I'll never take for granted."

magnificent meat

comforting stovetop short ribs

Serves 3-4

I know a lot of chefs whose signature dishes include short ribs. So I thought, why not help you bring out your chef side by giving you my recipe for short ribs? You're going to take this great cut of beef and make a great meal for your family. It's going to be comforting, full of flavor, and it's going to make you pretty popular at the dinner table.

¼ cup all-purpose flour

3-½ to 4 pounds beef short ribs

2 tablespoons olive oil

2 carrots, cut into 1-½-inch chunks

2 stalks celery, cut into 1-inch chunks

1 onion, cut into 1-inch chunks

2 sprigs fresh rosemary

2 teaspoons chopped garlic

2 cups beef broth

½ cup dry red wine

½ teaspoon salt

¼ teaspoon black pepper

❋ Place flour in a shallow dish, then evenly coat short ribs.

❋ In a soup pot over high heat, heat the oil until hot; sauté short ribs for 8 to 10 minutes or until all sides are browned.

❋ Drain oil from the pot. Add remaining ingredients; stir until well combined. Bring to a boil, cover, and reduce heat to medium-low. Simmer for 1-½ hours or until the ribs are fork-tender and meat is falling off the bones. Serve ribs in a shallow soup bowl with vegetables and broth.

Chef Tony's Tip: When you're slow cooking a dish like ribs or stew on the stovetop, I recommend using a heavy soup pot. A heavy soup pot helps retain the heat and prevents the ingredients on the bottom from getting scorched.

mama jeanie's special brisket

Serves 8-10

I had a friend named Marc who was more like an adopted brother to me. We grew up within 20 blocks of one another and spent a lot of time at each other's homes. His mom, whom we lovingly called "Mama Jeanie," was my Jewish mother. She reminded me so much of my own mother (whose own nickname was "Jeana"), and they got along fabulously. One of Mama Jeanie's specialties was her brisket. She made it with an amazing, savory sauce and lots of TLC.

Jeanie's Special Rub

¼ cup brown sugar

2 tablespoons paprika

1 teaspoon celery seed

2 tablespoons onion powder

2 tablespoons garlic powder

1 teaspoon ground mustard

1 teaspoon salt

1 teaspoon black pepper

1 (5- to 6-pound) beef brisket

3 onions, coarsely chopped

2 cups water

2 packages onion soup mix

✳ Preheat oven to 350 degrees F. In a small bowl, combine all the ingredients in Jeanie's Special Rub and mix well. With your hands, rub the mixture over the entire brisket.

✳ Place the onions in the bottom of a roasting pan. Place brisket over the onions. In a small bowl, combine the water and onion soup mix; mix well and pour over brisket. Cover tightly with aluminum foil.

✳ Roast about 3 hours or until fork-tender. Uncover, baste with pan drippings, and cook uncovered, for an additional 30 minutes to allow the top to get a bit more browned.

✳ Let rest for about 10 minutes, then slice brisket across the grain. Serve with the pan drippings and the melt-in-your-mouth onions.

low-and-slow beef stew

Serves 5-6

My family knows that when it comes to a rich beef stew like this, "low and slow is the only way to go!" When my kids had a test coming up or if I knew somebody had a bad day at school or at work, I'd get to work on making this. There are some things only a hearty bowl of stew can make better.

2 pounds beef stew meat

¼ cup all-purpose flour

1 teaspoon salt, divided

1 teaspoon black pepper, divided

3 cloves garlic, chopped

2 tablespoons Worcestershire sauce

½ teaspoon dried thyme leaf

4 potatoes, cut into 1-inch chunks

5 carrots, cut into 1-inch chunks

1 onion, cut into 1-inch chunks

2 celery stalks, sliced

1 (14-½-ounce) can diced tomatoes, undrained

1-¾ cups beef broth

✳ Trim beef stew meat to remove excess fat and cut into 1-inch pieces. (This will help it cook evenly.)

✳ In a large bowl, mix together the flour, ½ teaspoon salt, and ½ teaspoon pepper. Add the beef and toss until well coated.

✳ Place the beef in a 5-quart or larger slow cooker and top with the remaining ingredients. (Don't forget to add in the remaining ½ teaspoon each of salt and pepper!) Then, give it a stir.

✳ Cover and cook on LOW 9 to 10 hours or on HIGH 4 to 5 hours. Serve in a bowl and enjoy.

Chef Tony's Tip: Even though it's not necessary to brown the meat before adding it to the slow cooker, when time permits, I go ahead and do it. I think it adds a richer flavor to the finished stew. If you want to do it too, all you need to do is heat a large heavy skillet over medium-high heat, add a little vegetable oil, and sauté the beef until the outside is browned.

herb-crusted rib roast

Serves 6-8

Rib roast has always been a Christmas Day tradition in the Notaro house, alongside all of our other traditional Italian foods (like lasagna!). As my kids got older, they started asking for it on their birthdays too. So now, I guess you could say it's a special occasion and holiday tradition. A buttery, herb crust adds an amazing amount of flavor to this perfectly cooked roast.

1 (5-6 pound) boneless rib eye roast

1 stick salted butter, at room temp

1 teaspoon dried thyme leaf

1 teaspoon dried rosemary

1 teaspoon onion powder

1 tablespoon minced fresh garlic

½ teaspoon kosher salt

1 teaspoon black pepper

¼ cup dry red wine

¼ cup beef broth

✺ Preheat oven to 350 degrees F. Coat a metal roasting pan with cooking spray. Place the roast fat-side up on a rack in the roasting pan.

✺ In a small bowl, combine butter, thyme, rosemary, onion powder, garlic, salt, and pepper; mix well. Rub mixture evenly over the beef.

✺ Roast beef 30 minutes, then reduce heat to 300 degrees and continue to cook 1-½ to 2 hours for medium rare (135 degrees) or until desired doneness. Remove beef to cutting board and let rest 15 to 20 minutes. (This will help the beef retain its juices once it's cut.)

✺ Meanwhile, on the stovetop over medium heat, add wine and beef broth to the roasting pan (make sure the pan is stovetop safe) and deglaze it by whisking the pan drippings for 2 to 3 minutes. Carve the roast across the grain into ½-inch to 1-inch slices. Spoon the pan drippings over the beef and serve immediately.

Chef Tony's Tip: Sometimes, instead of using a roasting rack, I make a bed of vegetables (with celery, carrots, and onions) for the roast to sit on. This adds additional flavor to the roast while it cooks.

no reservations filet mignon

Serves 2

Filet mignon isn't something you have to make a reservation for. I can tell you, with confidence, that anyone can make this 5-star steak dinner at home. I make this recipe from time to time, as a special treat for Vivian and me, as we both love Parmesan cheese. We light a few candles, open up a good bottle of our favorite wine, and turn on some light music. It's a nice way for us to have a romantic evening at home.

½ stick butter, softened

¼ cup panko bread crumbs

¼ cup grated Parmesan cheese

1 tablespoon chopped
fresh chives

1 clove garlic, minced

¼ teaspoon salt

¼ teaspoon black pepper

2 beef filet mignons
(about 1-½-inch thick)

✵ In a medium bowl, combine butter, bread crumbs, Parmesan cheese, chives, garlic, salt, and pepper; mix well. Form the mixture into 2 (2-inch) round discs. Wrap them in plastic wrap and refrigerate at least 1 hour.

✵ Coat a grill pan or skillet with cooking spray; over medium-high heat, sear the filets for 4 to 5 minutes per side for medium-rare (145 degrees) or to desired doneness.

✵ Preheat the broiler to low setting. Place cooked steaks on a rimmed baking sheet and top each with a Parmesan disc. Broil for 3 to 5 minutes or until the cheese crust turns golden.

family-sized loaded meatball

Serves 4

If you want to test someone's skills as an Italian cook, ask them to make you meatballs. If their meatballs are fork tender and taste really good, then there's a pretty good chance they know their way around an Italian kitchen. This recipe takes me way back – it's the way my ma made meatballs for us when we were kids. I loved it then, I love it now, and I'm sure you and your family are going to love it too.

1 pound ground beef

3/4 cup plain bread crumbs

1/2 cup grated Parmesan cheese

1 egg

1 tablespoon chopped fresh parsley

1/2 cup water

1-1/2 teaspoons garlic powder

1 teaspoon salt

1/2 teaspoon black pepper

1 cup spaghetti sauce

3/4 cup ricotta cheese

1/2 cup shredded mozzarella cheese

- Preheat oven to 350 degrees F. Coat a 9-inch pie plate with cooking spray.
- In a large bowl, combine the beef, bread crumbs, Parmesan cheese, egg, parsley, water, garlic powder, salt, and pepper; gently mix until combined, but don't over-mix it or the meatball will be too dense. Form the mixture into one large meatball and place it in the pie plate. (It's going to be one big, shareable meatball!)
- Roast for 55 to 60 minutes or until juices run clear.
- Place 1/2 cup of spaghetti sauce in the bottom of a 1-1/2-quart casserole dish. Place the meatball on the sauce and cut it into quarters (as shown). Dollop the ricotta cheese into the center, and spoon the remaining spaghetti sauce over the cheese and the quartered meatball. Sprinkle the sauce with mozzarella cheese and place meatball in the oven for 5 minutes or until the cheese is melted.

Chef Tony's Tip: In my house, this family-sized meatball is always served with a side of spaghetti. It puts a whole new spin on spaghetti and meatballs!

really juicy cheeseburgers

Serves 6

Like Popeye's friend Wimpy, I love hamburgers. I really like ones that you can sink your teeth into; that you need two hands to hold on to. I also like them to be really juicy – so juicy that you need extra napkins. This one really fits my criteria! While I don't always have a burger in my hand, I do eat them at least once a week. Now, get ready for the best burger you've ever tasted!

2 pounds ground chuck

4 ounces cheddar cheese, diced

¼ cup real bacon bits

2 teaspoons Worcestershire sauce

2 tablespoons ketchup

1 teaspoon mustard

2 tablespoons water

½ teaspoon garlic powder

½ teaspoon salt

½ teaspoon black pepper

6 hamburger buns, split

✵ In a large bowl, combine all ingredients except buns; mix just until combined, then shape mixture into 6 equal-sized patties. Make an indentation in the center of each burger with your thumb. (See Tip.) (If you aren't serving 6 people, wrap up the patties you won't be cooking and freeze them, so that you have them for another time.)

✵ Heat a large skillet or grill pan over medium-high heat and cook the patties 4 to 5 minutes per side or until desired doneness. (If you have an instant read thermometer, the temperature should be 145 degrees for medium-rare, or to desired doneness.) Place the patties in the buns and serve.

Chef Tony's Tip: The reason for making an indentation in the burger patty is that it prevents it from puffing up while it cooks. The last thing we want is for our hamburgers to look like meatballs.

cornbread-topped chili bake

Serves 6-8

When it gets cold in the winter, no one wants to go outside. That's when I bake this heart-and body-warming, all-in-one chili dish. First, everyone gathers around the table to fill their bellies, then it's on to some of our favorite board games. In the end, a cold winter day turns into a memorable, family-fun night.

2 tablespoons vegetable oil

1 large onion, chopped

3 cloves garlic, minced

2 pounds ground beef

1 teaspoon instant coffee granules

1 (28-ounce) can crushed tomatoes, undrained

2 tablespoons chili powder

1 teaspoon ground cumin

1 teaspoon salt

1 teaspoon black pepper

2 (16-ounce) cans red kidney beans, drained well

1 (8.5-ounce) package corn muffin mix

✵ In a large pot over medium-high heat, heat oil until hot; sauté the onion and garlic for 3 to 4 minutes or until tender. (Be careful not to burn the garlic.) Add the beef and brown 8 to 10 minutes or until no pink remains. (Make sure you break up the beef with a wooden spoon, so that it's evenly crumbled.) Drain any excess liquid.

✵ Add remaining ingredients except the muffin mix; mix well. (If you're wondering why I add the coffee to the mixture, I think it gives it some extra richness and body.) Cover and simmer over low heat 20 to 25 minutes or until thickened.

✵ Preheat oven to 375 degrees F. Coat a 9- x 13-inch baking dish with cooking spray. Spoon chili into the baking dish. Prepare muffin batter as directed on package; spread over chili. Bake 20 minutes or until the cornbread topping sets. Cool slightly and serve by the spoonful.

Chef Tony's Tip: Sprinkle the top with some shredded cheddar or Monterey Jack cheese right when it comes out of the oven, to add a little cheesiness to the dish. The warmth from the cornbread will melt it in no time.

mashed potato "stuffed" meatloaf

Serves 5-6

My aunt Nancy made stuffed meatloaves all the time, and they were amazing. She's probably the reason why I turned stuffed meatloaf into a personal challenge. Over the years, I've come up with dozens of ways to stuff meatloaf. If I had leftovers, into a meatloaf they went. To this day, I've made stuffed meatloaf with mac 'n' cheese, manicotti, enchiladas, roasted veggies...you name it! Here's one I came up with using some leftover mashed potatoes.

1-½ pounds ground beef

¾ cup Italian bread crumbs

½ cup finely chopped onion

1 egg

½ cup water

1 teaspoon garlic powder

1 teaspoon salt

½ teaspoon black pepper

3 slices provolone cheese

¾ cup fresh spinach leaves, stems removed

1 (12-ounce) jar roasted red peppers, drained well and cut into strips

2 cups leftover mashed potatoes (see Tip)

✳ Preheat oven to 350 degrees F. Coat a 9- x 5-inch loaf pan with cooking spray.

✳ In a large bowl, combine the beef, bread crumbs, onion, egg, water, garlic powder, salt, and pepper; mix well. Press the meat mixture evenly into the bottom and up the sides of the loaf pan, creating a "well" in the center. (Check out the photo to see what I mean!)

✳ Line the well with provolone cheese. Top with spinach, and place the roasted peppers over the spinach. Then spread the mashed potatoes over the entire top, as shown.

✳ Roast for 60 to 70 minutes or until juices run clear and the peaks of the potatoes turn golden. Allow to set for 5 to 10 minutes before slicing.

Chef Tony's Tip: You don't have to wait until you have leftover mashed potatoes to make this. You can use store-bought, refrigerated, mashed potatoes when you're in a time crunch or, if time permits, whip up your own from scratch.

your way sausage, peppers, & onions

Serves 3-4

For those of you who've seen my presentation of Annabelle's Kitchen sausage on QVC, you already know that rope sausage is very dear to me. Not only is it the first food item I ever sold on QVC, but it's really tasty, and our family's first choice... hands down! Inspired by a presentation one day, I came home and whipped up this flavorful dish. It's good on anything from a crusty roll to serving on top of pasta or pizza. Enjoy it your way!

3 tablespoons vegetable oil

2 green bell peppers, cut into ½-inch strips

2 red bell peppers, cut into ½-inch strips

1 large onion, cut into ¼-inch slices

½ teaspoon salt

1 pound mild Italian rope sausage, cut into 3-inch pieces

¼ cup dark beer (optional)

✹ In a large skillet over medium heat, heat oil until hot.

✹ Add the peppers, onion, and salt; cook 8 to 10 minutes or until tender, stirring occasionally.

✹ Place the sausage over the veggies and cook 10 to 15 more minutes or until sausage is no longer pink in center, stirring occasionally. Add the beer, if desired, and simmer 2 to 3 minutes or until it cooks down.

Chef Tony's Tip: I like to serve this with, or on, a crusty Italian roll. Add a sprinkle of Parmesan and hold on taste buds... here it comes!

lip-smacking country-style ribs

Serves 4-6

Country-style ribs are really meaty, more so than traditional pork ribs, which means that you get a lot more bang for your buck. And when you cook them in a really flavorful sauce, like I do in this recipe, you can be sure that no one is leaving anything on their plates. Actually, you might catch some people licking their fingers, smacking their lips, or throwing glances at the pot (wondering, "Is there more?").

2 tablespoons vegetable oil

4-5 pounds country-style pork ribs

1 (12-ounce) bottle chili sauce

½ cup water

2 tablespoons Worcestershire sauce

1 tablespoon yellow mustard

¼ cup brown sugar

❋ In a heavy soup pot over medium-high heat, heat oil until hot. Sear the ribs for 8 to 10 minutes or until all sides are browned.

❋ Meanwhile, in a large bowl, combine the remaining ingredients; mix well.

❋ Reduce heat to medium and drain off the pan drippings. Pour the sauce mixture over the ribs, cover loosely, and cook 1-½ hours or until ribs are fork-tender, turning occasionally. Serve slathered with sauce.

Chef Tony's Tip: If you want to serve these at a cookout, after they're cooked per the instructions above, place the ribs on the grill just long enough to get the grill marks. Or if you want to add a nice light crust in the wintertime, just broil them for a couple of minutes in the oven.

pork chops 'n' potato bake

Serves 4

I've got another all-in-one recipe for you, and this one is going to be a favorite for all of you "meat and potatoes" foodies out there (I'm one of you too!). With this one, you'll get juicy pork chops and comforting, buttery, scalloped potatoes. To make sure you get some green veggies into your meal, serve it with a fresh green salad. Dinner is done!

4 russet potatoes, thinly sliced

4 tablespoons butter, divided

3 tablespoons all-purpose flour

1 teaspoon salt

¼ teaspoon black pepper

2 cups chicken broth

4 boneless pork chops (about ¾ inches thick)

1 onion, thinly sliced

Paprika for sprinkling

❋ Place potatoes in a medium saucepan and add enough water to cover them. Bring to a boil over medium-high heat; cook for 6 to 7 minutes or until fork-tender. Drain well.

❋ Meanwhile, in another medium saucepan over medium heat, melt 3 tablespoons butter. Add the flour, salt, and pepper, and cook for 1 minute, stirring constantly. Whisk in the broth and bring to a boil, then set aside.

❋ In a large skillet over medium-high heat, melt remaining 1 tablespoon butter. Add the pork chops and cook for 1 to 2 minutes per side or until browned; remove to a plate. Add onion slices to the skillet and sauté for 3 to 4 minutes or until just tender.

❋ Preheat oven to 350 degrees F. Coat a 9- x 13-inch baking dish with cooking spray.

❋ Place potatoes evenly in the baking dish and top with onion. Pour broth mixture over onion and potatoes. Top with pork chops and cover with aluminum foil.

❋ Roast for 15 minutes. Uncover, sprinkle with paprika, and cook for another 20 to 25 minutes or until pork is at least 145 degrees (for medium) or until desired doneness, and potatoes are heated through.

apples & pork chops

Serves 4

When my kids were still kids, I used to take them to pick apples in some of the orchards in Michigan. They loved doing it, but they especially loved eating all of the apple treats after we were done. Since we'd go home with baskets full of apples, it was left up to me to come up with some ways to use them. One easy way was to cook them down and pair them up with pork chops; it's a classic combination that tastes great.

4 (1-inch) bone-in pork loin chops

½ teaspoon salt

¼ teaspoon black pepper

¼ cup all-purpose flour

¼ cup vegetable oil

2 Granny Smith apples, peeled, cored, and diced

½ cup chopped onion

½ cup apple cider

❋ Sprinkle pork chops evenly with salt and pepper. Place flour in a shallow dish. Dip chops in flour, coating completely.

❋ In a large deep skillet over medium heat, heat oil until hot. Add chops and cook 6 to 8 minutes per side for medium (145 degrees) or to desired doneness. Remove to a serving plate; cover to keep warm.

❋ Add the apples and onion to the same skillet and sauté for 2 to 3 minutes or until tender. Add the apple cider, stir well, and simmer 3 to 5 minutes or until the mixture thickens.

❋ Spoon the apple mixture over the chops and enjoy.

Chef Tony's Tip: Since I love apples, I often serve these chops with a small crock of apple butter for dipping. It adds some extra yumminess.

weeknight easy pork tenderloin

Serves 3-4

Take a peek into my freezer on any day of the week, and you're sure to find a pork tenderloin in there. I always keep them in the house because it's one of my favorite proteins to work with. They're quick, simple, and cook up nice and tender. In this recipe, I went with a combo of mushrooms and onions that works perfectly with the pork.

2 tablespoons all-purpose flour

½ teaspoon salt

⅛ teaspoon black pepper

1 (14- to 16-ounce) pork tenderloin

3 tablespoons olive oil

½ pound sliced fresh mushrooms

2 onions, thinly sliced

½ cup beef or chicken broth

✳ In a shallow dish, combine the flour, salt, and pepper; mix well. Coat the pork tenderloin with this mixture.

✳ In a large heavy skillet or Dutch oven over medium-high heat, heat oil until hot. Add tenderloin and cook 6 to 8 minutes, turning frequently to ensure all sides are brown. Remove to a platter and set aside.

✳ In the same skillet, add the mushrooms and onions and sauté 6 to 8 minutes or until tender, stirring occasionally. Stir in the broth, return tenderloin to the skillet, and cook 5 to 6 minutes or until desired doneness (See Tip.) and the sauce starts to thicken.

✳ Carve tenderloin into ½-inch slices. Serve topped with the mushrooms and onions.

Chef Tony's Tip: When it comes to pork (especially cuts like tenderloin, chops, and loin roasts), you don't want to overcook it. It's recommended that pork be cooked to a minimum internal temperature of 145 degrees (medium rare). (It's not necessary to cook it until it's like shoe leather anymore.) By taking care not to overcook it, you can bet that every bite is going to be juicy!

memorable veal caprese

Serves 4

Mamma mia, this is my favorite dish that my mom made for me. When I lived in Las Vegas, and I'd fly back east to visit her, I'd ask if she could make this dish for me. She always said yes. And every time she made it, she made it with lots of love. To this day, it still brings me to tears (of joy and sorrow) knowing that this dish was the last thing that my mom made for me before she passed away. Ma, I love you!

1 egg

1 tablespoon water

¾ cup Italian bread crumbs

3 tablespoons olive oil

4 veal cutlets (about 1 pound)

1 (8-ounce) ball fresh mozzarella cheese, cut into 8 slices

12 slices plum tomatoes

¼ cup pesto sauce

✳ Preheat oven to 400 degrees F. In a shallow dish, whisk the egg and water. Place bread crumbs in another shallow dish.

✳ In a large skillet over medium heat, heat oil until hot. Dip veal cutlets in the egg mixture, then place in the bread crumbs, coating evenly on both sides. Cook veal in batches for 2 minutes per side or until golden brown.

✳ Place veal on a baking sheet. Top each cutlet with 2 slices of cheese and 3 slices of tomato. Place in oven for 2 to 4 minutes or until cheese is slightly melted. Drizzle with pesto sauce and serve immediately.

chef Tony's Tip: Make sure that the veal is cut very thin; this way it will be nice and tender. (To do this, place each piece between some plastic wrap and use a meat mallet to pound it until it's thin.) I also make this same dish using chicken cutlets.

garlic and herb lamb chops

Serves 3-4

Fancy schmancy? ... Nah! Although a lot of people think of lamb as too fancy to make themselves, I'm here to tell you that's not true. As a big fan of lamb, I cook it pretty often. It's no more work than cooking any other kind of meat and the flavor is phenomenal. To get you started, here's a simple recipe that has a whole lot of herb goodness going on.

1 tablespoon fresh rosemary leaves

1 teaspoon fresh thyme leaves

2 sprigs fresh parsley

2 cloves fresh garlic

1/4 teaspoon salt

1/8 teaspoon black pepper

1/4 cup olive oil

8 lamb rib chops

❁ In a food processor or blender, pulse the rosemary, thyme, parsley, garlic, salt, and pepper until combined. Pour in oil and pulse until thoroughly combined. Pour the mixture into a shallow dish.

❁ Add chops to mixture and toss until evenly coated. Cover and refrigerate for at least 1 hour. (The longer they sit in the marinade, the better. However, I suggest no longer than 2 days.)

❁ In a grill pan or large skillet over medium-high heat, sear the chops for 2 minutes, then turn over and cook for another 3 to 5 minutes or to desired doneness (145 degrees for medium-rare). Serve immediately, with pan drippings.

"When I was a kid, the fishing boats would pull into an inlet near our house. Every Friday afternoon my parents and I would walk along the bay and buy the freshest fish available."

sensational seafood

colossal stuffed shrimp

Serves 4-5

Take a deep breath and let all the pressures of the day disappear. Then go ahead and make yourself this shrimp dish for dinner. It'll help you get into a new and relaxed mood – at least it always does for me. Serve it with something extra comforting like buttery mashed potatoes, and you'll be feeling great in no time at all.

½ pound lump crabmeat, flaked (see Tip)

½ cup Italian bread crumbs

1 celery stalk, finely chopped

3 tablespoons mayonnaise

1 teaspoon Worcestershire sauce

1 teaspoon lemon juice

½ teaspoon onion powder

½ teaspoon black pepper

1 pound colossal raw shrimp, peeled and deveined (13-15 per pound)

2 slices prosciutto (Italian ham)

✳ Preheat oven to 450 degrees F. Coat a baking sheet with cooking spray.

✳ In a medium bowl, combine crabmeat, bread crumbs, celery, mayonnaise, Worcestershire sauce, lemon juice, onion powder, and pepper; mix well. Place shrimp on their sides, on baking sheet. Mound a heaping tablespoon of crabmeat mixture onto each shrimp and gently press it down so it stays in place.

✳ Bake 8 to 10 minutes or until shrimp turn pink.

✳ Meanwhile, in a large skillet over high heat, pan sear the prosciutto until crispy. Then remove and allow to cool on a plate. Right before serving, crumble the prosciutto and sprinkle over the shrimp.

Chef Tony's Tip: Although I love the taste and texture of lump crabmeat, I have been known to use imitation crab on occasion, simply based on the price. It's a lot cheaper and the results are amazing.

pan-fried fish & crispy potato wedges

Serves 4

I've eaten more than my fair share of fish and chips during my trips to QVC London. It's a must-have! Now, I'm sharing a recipe for you to make this classic British favorite at home. Traditionally, this dish is cooked in a deep fryer, but I prefer to use a regular frying pan for my fish, and the oven for my "chips." You still end up with the same flaky, crispy, goodness, but with a whole lot less oil.

½ cup vegetable oil, divided

1 teaspoon seasoning salt

½ teaspoon black pepper, divided

4 baking potatoes, cut into wedges

¾ cup yellow cornmeal

1 cup instant potato flakes

½ teaspoon salt

4 (6-ounce) cod or haddock fillets

½ stick butter, melted

✹ Preheat oven to 450 degrees F.

✹ In a large bowl, combine ¼ cup oil, the seasoning salt, and ¼ teaspoon black pepper. Add the potato wedges and toss until evenly coated. Place on a baking sheet. Bake 25 to 30 minutes or until golden and crispy.

✹ Meanwhile, in a shallow dish, combine cornmeal, potato flakes, salt, and remaining ¼ teaspoon pepper. Dip fish in melted butter, then dredge in the cornmeal mixture.

✹ In a large skillet over medium-high heat, heat remaining ¼ cup oil until hot; add fish and fry 4 to 6 minutes per side or until it flakes easily with a fork. Drain on paper towels. Serve with crispy potato wedges.

Chef Tony's Tip: Make sure you add a bottle of malt vinegar to your shopping list before making this. A shake or two on the fish and chips is just heavenly.

Sensational Seafood

celebration seafood fra diavolo

Serves 6-8

There's no question about it; this is a special occasion kind of meal. We could always tell we were celebrating something special when Mom would come home with all kinds of fresh seafood. (We knew it was EXTRA-special if there was lobster!) No matter what she tossed in, it was always a hit. It made every celebratory occasion even better. So if you want to impress someone or celebrate something great, I suggest you make this tongue-tingling dish!

3 tablespoons olive oil

4 cloves garlic, coarsely chopped

1 (28-ounce) can crushed tomatoes, undrained

1 (28-ounce) can diced tomatoes, undrained

2 tablespoons dried oregano

1 teaspoon dried basil

1 teaspoon sugar

1 teaspoon crushed red pepper

1-½ teaspoons salt

½ teaspoon black pepper

1 dozen little neck clams, cleaned

1 pound large shrimp, peeled, deveined, and tails removed

½ pound bay scallops

1 pound spaghetti

❋ In a large pot over medium heat, heat the oil until hot; sauté the garlic for 2 to 3 minutes or until golden. (Be careful you don't burn it!)

❋ Stir in the crushed and diced tomatoes (with their juice), the oregano, basil, sugar, red pepper, salt, and black pepper. Reduce the heat to low, cover, and simmer for 25 to 30 minutes.

❋ Add the clams to the pot; cover and cook for 5 minutes. Add the shrimp and scallops, and cook an additional 5 to 7 minutes or until the clams have opened and the shrimp are pink.

❋ Meanwhile, cook the spaghetti according to the package directions; drain. Discard any unopened clams, then serve the seafood and sauce over the pasta and enjoy.

Chef Tony's Tip: Feel free to mix and match the seafood. Maybe replace clams with mussels or replace the shrimp with cut-up lobster tail. You get the idea!

teriyaki-glazed salmon packets

Serves 4

Better-for-you definitely doesn't mean boring-for-you, and this recipe is proof of that - just ask any of one my kids! They loved when I would make foil packet dinners like this, because it was like opening up a tasty surprise. Inside these packets you'll find perfectly cooked salmon with yummy, Asian-inspired flavors. Even your picky eaters will dig into this!

4 (4-ounce) salmon fillets

¼ teaspoon ground ginger

¼ teaspoon garlic powder

¼ teaspoon salt

¼ teaspoon black pepper

1 scallion, sliced

1 tablespoon sesame oil

¼ cup teriyaki sauce

1 tablespoon honey

½ teaspoon cornstarch

Sesame seeds for sprinkling

✳ Preheat oven to 375 degrees F. Place 4 pieces of aluminum foil (each about 8-inches long), on your counter and coat with cooking spray. Place a salmon fillet on each piece of foil.

✳ In a small bowl, combine ginger, garlic powder, salt, and pepper; mix well. Evenly sprinkle seasoning mixture over the salmon, then top with sliced scallions, and a drizzle of sesame oil. Loosely fold up foil, making a packet. (Make sure you seal the edges tightly, so there is room for steam to build up in the foil packets while they're in the oven.) Place the foil packets on a baking sheet.

✳ Bake for 15 to 20 minutes or until fish flakes easily with a fork.

✳ Meanwhile, in a small microwave-safe bowl, whisk together the teriyaki sauce, honey, and cornstarch until combined. Microwave for 1-1/2 to 2 minutes or until thickened. Carefully open the foil packets (they will be very hot inside), drizzle with the glaze, and sprinkle with sesame seeds. Serve immediately.

Chef Tony's Tip: If available, I recommend buying wild salmon. The flavor and texture are amazing! Or, try this with other firm fish like, cod, halibut, mahi-mahi, or tilapia.

crab-topped tilapia fillets

Makes 6

Is someone feeling a little crabby at home? Cheer them up by making this fancy restaurant-style dinner. There's no need to go out or to spend a ton of money. All you need are a few simple ingredients and an extra dash of love. Before you know it, you'll have transformed your dining room into a wonderful seaside eatery, and it all starts with this dish.

½ pound real crabmeat, flaked

½ cup Italian panko bread crumbs

½ teaspoon onion powder

¼ teaspoon garlic powder

1 teaspoon chopped fresh parsley

1 tablespoon chopped shallots

½ stick butter, melted

6 (6-ounce) tilapia fillets

✳ Preheat oven to 350 degrees F. Coat a baking sheet with cooking spray.

✳ In a medium bowl, combine all ingredients except tilapia; gently mix, so you don't break up the crabmeat.

✳ Place tilapia on the baking sheet and evenly divide the stuffing mixture onto each fillet. Bake 15 to 20 minutes or until fish flakes easily. Serve immediately.

Chef Tony's Tip: Don't forget to add a squeeze of fresh lemon at the end. It gives this an extra blast of flavor!.

pan-seared scallops & wilted spinach

Serves 3-4

As you may know, I didn't graduate from a culinary school – my parents just couldn't it afford it at the time. But that didn't stop me from learning how to cook and mastering the art of cooking flashy dishes like this. I just did it the old-fashioned way; I read a lot of cookbooks, underlined the important stuff, and put it to practice. Now it's my pleasure to help you make something amazing, like these pan-seared scallops!

1 pound large fresh or frozen and thawed scallops, patted dry

½ teaspoon salt, divided

½ teaspoon black pepper, divided

3 tablespoons butter

3 tablespoons olive oil, divided

½ cup chopped onion

4 cloves garlic, minced

1 cup cherry or grape tomatoes, cut in half

¼ cup white wine

1 tablespoon capers

1 (16-ounce) package fresh spinach

✳ Sprinkle scallops evenly with ¼ teaspoon salt and ¼ teaspoon pepper. In a large skillet (preferably NOT non-stick) over medium-high heat, melt butter. Sauté the scallops 3 to 4 minutes per side or until golden and the center is firm. (You'll know the scallops are ready to flip when they easily release from the skillet). Remove to a platter and cover to keep warm.

✳ In the same skillet over medium-high heat, heat 2 tablespoons oil until hot; cook the onion, garlic, tomatoes, and remaining ¼ teaspoon salt and ¼ teaspoon pepper 4 to 5 minutes or until onion is soft. Stir in the wine and capers and continue cooking 3 to 5 minutes or until heated through.

✳ Meanwhile, in another skillet, heat remaining 1 tablespoon oil. Add spinach and cook 1 to 2 minutes or until it begins to wilt.

✳ To serve, place the wilted spinach on a plate, top with scallops, and spoon the sauce over it.

shrimp scampi with yellow rice

Serves 4-5

Shrimp scampi isn't anything new, but the idea of cooking it in the oven (versus sauléing it in a pan) is a little out of the ordinary (just like me!). Cooking it this way results in a richer, nuttier flavor that's just really irresistible. I serve this over yellow rice because it's one of my favorites. Plus, I love seeing the contrasting colors on my plate!

1 stick butter

10 cloves garlic, minced

1 teaspoon salt

½ teaspoon black pepper

1 pound large shrimp, peeled and deveined, with tails left on

½ cup white wine

1 tablespoon chopped fresh parsley

½ fresh lemon, squeezed

3 cups cooked yellow rice, warmed

❀ Preheat oven to 425 degrees F.

❀ Place the butter, garlic, salt, and pepper in a 9- x 13-inch baking dish, and heat in oven for 5 to 7 minutes or until butter is melted. Remove from oven and add the shrimp, wine, and parsley; stir to coat shrimp.

❀ Return to oven and roast for 6 to 8 minutes or until shrimp are pink and cooked through. Stir shrimp mixture, then drizzle with lemon juice. Serve over yellow rice.

Chef Tony's Tip: Did you know that you can buy pre-cooked yellow rice? It's typically sold in pouches, right in the rice aisle. All you have to do is heat these up in the microwave and they're ready to serve!

"Someone once told my mom that my pasta was better than hers. She didn't talk to me for six months! Finally, a couple years later, she tasted mine and said,
"How can I make mine taste like yours?"

pasta & more

one-pot
pasta dinner

Serves 4-6

Even the best cooks need shortcut recipes in their arsenal. Here you've got everything cooking together in just one pot, so you're not juggling a bunch of pots and pans (and whoever washes the dishes at your house won't be complaining either). This spaghetti dish, loaded with greens and other fresh veggies, is the perfect weeknight dinner choice – it's quick, it's tasty, and it's very easy.

12 ounces spaghetti, uncooked, broken in half

1 (28-ounce) can diced tomatoes, undrained

1 onion, thinly sliced

2 cups quartered mushrooms

3 cups shredded kale

4 cloves garlic, thinly sliced

5 cups chicken or vegetable broth

2 teaspoons dried oregano

½ teaspoon crushed red pepper flakes (optional)

½ teaspoon salt

2 tablespoons olive oil

Grated Parmesan cheese for sprinkling

✳ In a soup pot, place the spaghetti, tomatoes with their liquid, onion, mushrooms, kale, and garlic. Pour in the broth and sprinkle with oregano, crushed red pepper, if desired, and salt; mix well. Drizzle with oil and cover.

✳ Over medium heat, bring to a boil. Reduce heat to low, and simmer for 10 minutes, stirring every 2 to 3 minutes or until most of the liquid is absorbed (but not to the point where there's no liquid left). Serve each bowl with a little Parmesan cheese sprinkled on top.

Chef Tony's Tip: To get the most flavor from your Parmesan cheese, grate it right over the top of your dish. An inexpensive rasp grater is a kitchen tool that makes this a breeze.

old world
pasta bolognese

Serves 4-6

Some people think that Bolognese just means sauce with meat, but I'll go ahead and tell you that a good Bolognese is made with lots of meat and a little sauce (not the other way around!). This dish is all about the Bolognese. It's simple, but it's true to itself. I think you'll agree that, with a dish like this, simple is often better.

½ pound ground beef

½ pound ground pork

1 carrot, shredded

1 onion, chopped

1 green bell pepper, chopped

1 tablespoon chopped garlic

½ teaspoon salt

½ teaspoon black pepper

1 (15-ounce) can tomato sauce

1 (14.5-ounce) can diced tomatoes, undrained

1 teaspoon dried oregano

1 pound ziti

Basil for garnish

❋ In a large pot over medium-high heat, brown the beef and pork for 5 to 7 minutes. Drain excess liquid, then add the carrot, onion, green pepper, garlic, salt, and black pepper. Cook for 4 to 5 minutes or until vegetables are tender, stirring occasionally.

❋ Add the tomato sauce, diced tomatoes with their liquid, and oregano; loosely cover, and reduce heat to low. Simmer 20 minutes, stirring occasionally.

❋ Meanwhile, cook the pasta according to package directions; drain and place in a large serving bowl.

❋ Spoon sauce over pasta, garnish with basil, and serve immediately.

my childhood lasagna

Serves 8-10

This is the lasagna recipe that I grew up with. When I had kids of my own, I would have them in the kitchen with me as I made it. Not only was it a fun family activity, but it was a good way to teach them how to make it. Now that they are grown, I am so proud that they can carry on this special family tradition.

12 lasagna noodles

½ pound bulk Italian sausage

½ pound ground beef

½ cup chopped onion

4 cups shredded mozzarella cheese, divided

1 (15-ounce) container ricotta cheese

⅓ cup grated Parmesan cheese

1 teaspoon garlic powder

½ teaspoon dried basil

½ teaspoon black pepper

1 egg

2 (28-ounce) jars spaghetti sauce

Chef Tony's Tip: Rather than using store-bought sauce, you can use 6 cups of My Go-To Marinara Sauce on page 146. It's worth the extra time... I promise!

✱ Preheat oven to 375 degrees F. Coat a 9- x 13-inch baking dish with cooking spray. Cook lasagna noodles according to package directions; drain and set aside.

✱ Meanwhile, in a large skillet over medium-high heat, cook the sausage, ground beef, and onion until no pink remains in the meat, stirring to break up the meat as it cooks. Drain excess liquid and set aside in a bowl to cool slightly.

✱ In a medium bowl, combine 3 cups mozzarella cheese, the ricotta and Parmesan cheeses, garlic powder, basil, and pepper; mix well. (This is when I would taste it to see if it needs more seasoning.) Add egg and mix well.

✱ Spread 1 cup spaghetti sauce over bottom of the baking dish. Place 3 cooked noodles over sauce. Spread 1/3 of cheese mixture over noodles; sprinkle with 1/3 of the meat mixture. Pour 1 cup spaghetti sauce over meat mixture. Place 3 more noodles on top and press down lightly. Repeat with 2 more layers of cheese mixture, meat, sauce, and noodles. Spoon remaining sauce over top and cover tightly with aluminum foil.

✱ Bake for 1 hour or until bubbly and hot in center. Remove foil and top with the remaining 1 cup mozzarella cheese; return to oven 5 more minutes or until cheese has melted. Allow to sit 10 to 15 minutes before cutting and serving.

pepperoni spaghetti pie

Serves 6-8

Since my mom was always cooking for a crowd (we were a BIG family!), she would often look for new ways to serve up leftovers. Using leftover cooked pasta, along with some sauce and cheese, she created this "pie." It was a big hit! Today, I make it with sliced pepperoni or sliced meatballs, depending on my mood. I also serve each slice with some extra sauce, 'cause that's how she did it.

1 tablespoon olive oil

½ cup chopped onion

3 eggs

1 cup ricotta cheese

½ cup grated Parmesan cheese

1 teaspoon garlic powder

2 cups spaghetti sauce, divided

½ cup sliced pepperoni, chopped, plus 10 whole slices reserved for garnish

1 pound spaghetti, cooked according to package directions

1 cup shredded mozzarella cheese

✳ Preheat oven to 350 degrees F.

✳ In a large cast iron skillet over medium-high heat, heat oil until hot. Sauté the onion for 5 minutes or until tender; remove to a small bowl.

✳ In a large bowl, whisk the eggs. Add the ricotta cheese, Parmesan cheese, garlic powder, and 1 cup spaghetti sauce; mix well. Add the chopped pepperoni, onion, and spaghetti, and toss until evenly coated. Spoon evenly into the cast iron skillet, and top with remaining 1 cup spaghetti sauce.

✳ Bake for 45 minutes, then sprinkle with mozzarella cheese, garnish with pepperoni slices, and bake an additional 5 to 10 minutes or until cheese is melted. Let sit 10 minutes before slicing into wedges.

hot 'n' hearty tortellini stew

Serves 6-8

Stews like this are meant to be eaten immediately after they're done cooking, while they're still hot. That way you get the whole belly-warming experience with every spoonful. This reminds me of a story – whenever my grandma would make pasta with sauce, it would have to go from pot to plate instantly if she expected my grandpa to eat it. She'd have to sauce it on the plate or grandpa wouldn't touch it. He liked his meals hot and fresh.

1 (10-ounce) package Italian sausage, casings removed

1 large onion, chopped

3 cloves garlic, chopped

2 chicken breasts, diced

2 cups chicken broth

2 cups frozen mixed vegetables, thawed

1 (28-ounce) can crushed tomatoes with basil, undrained

½ teaspoon salt

¼ teaspoon black pepper

1 (16.9-ounce) package cheese tortellini, cooked according to package directions

¼ cup chopped fresh basil

✳ In a soup pot over medium-high heat, combine the sausage, onion, and garlic, and cook for 4 to 5 minutes or until sausage is browned, stirring occasionally. Add the chicken and cook for 4 to 5 minutes or until no longer pink.

✳ Add the broth, vegetables, tomatoes, salt, and pepper; bring to a boil. Reduce heat to low, add the cooked tortellini and basil, and simmer for 5 minutes. Serve immediately.

Chef Tony's Tip: This is a thick and rich-flavored stew that will stick to your ribs, but if you let it sit too long the pasta will start to absorb the sauce. If that happens, just add some water to it so it doesn't get too dry.

weekday eggplant parmigiana

Serves 4-5

Making eggplant parmigiana has always been somewhat of a time consuming chore. (First you've got to fry the eggplant, then you've got to build the layers, and then there's the baking.) Most of the time, I don't mind doing it, since I love eggplant parm so much, but whenever time is short, I make it this way instead. You get to skip the frying and layering steps, and still end up with the same great taste!

½ cup plain bread crumbs

1 tablespoon grated Parmesan cheese

1 teaspoon dried oregano

¼ cup all-purpose flour

2 eggs, lightly beaten

1 large eggplant, trimmed and cut lengthwise into ¼-inch slices (about 9 slices)

Cooking spray

1 cup spaghetti sauce

¾ cup finely shredded mozzarella cheese

✸ Preheat oven to 350 degrees F. Coat 2 large rimmed baking sheets with cooking spray.

✸ In a shallow dish, combine the bread crumbs, Parmesan cheese, and oregano; mix well. In another shallow dish, place the flour. In a third shallow dish, place the eggs.

✸ Dip eggplant slices in flour, then egg, then bread crumb mixture, coating completely with each. Arrange the eggplant slices in a single layer on the baking sheets. Lightly coat the tops of the eggplant with cooking spray. (Spraying the eggplant will help it get crispy as it bakes.) Bake for 25 to 30 minutes or until golden.

✸ Spoon the spaghetti sauce evenly over the baked eggplant slices, then sprinkle with mozzarella cheese. Bake for 8 to 10 additional minutes or until the cheese is melted. Serve immediately.

Chef Tony's Tip: Did you know that there are male and female eggplants? Male eggplants tend to have fewer seeds and are typically less bitter. To tell the difference between the two, turn them upside down! Male eggplants have a round dimple on the bottom, whereas female eggplants have more of an oval one. I know... it sounds crazy, right? Papa Frank taught me this and he knew his fruit and veggies!

ham & cheese
mac & cheese

Serves 5-6

I like my mac and cheese creamy, gooey, and topped with something crunchy. That's why I make mine with three different types of cheeses and generously sprinkle the top with crispy potato chips. If you don't fall in love with this recipe the way my family does every time I make it, then... well, I've never heard of anyone NOT loving this!

1 pound cavatappi pasta

5 tablespoons butter, divided

2 tablespoons all-purpose flour

½ teaspoon salt

½ teaspoon black pepper

3 cups milk

3 cups shredded sharp cheddar cheese

2 cups shredded Monterey Jack cheese

1-½ cups diced ham

½ pound mozzarella cheese, cut into ¼-inch cubes

¾ cup coarsely crushed potato chips

✳ Preheat oven to 350 degrees F. Coat a 2-½-quart baking dish with cooking spray.

✳ In a soup pot, cook the pasta according to package directions; drain and set aside.

✳ In the same pot over medium heat, melt 4 tablespoons butter. Add the flour, salt, and pepper; stir to mix well and let cook 1 minute, stirring constantly. Gradually whisk in the milk and cook until thickened, stirring constantly. Stir in the cheddar and Monterey Jack cheeses, and cook until melted. Return pasta to the pot along with the ham and mozzarella cheese. Mix well, then spoon mixture into the baking dish.

✳ In a small bowl, melt the remaining 1 tablespoon butter. Add the potato chips and stir to combine. Sprinkle over pasta and cheese. Bake uncovered for 35 to 40 minutes or until golden and bubbly.

Chef Tony's Tip: Get creative with your pasta shapes. Sometimes I make this with shells, other times with ziti. There's no wrong way!

my go-to
marinara sauce

Makes 8 cups

Learning my mom's recipes wasn't easy. Take for instance the time I decided to learn how to make my mom's amazing marinara sauce. I said to her, "Mom, I want you to teach me that recipe." She said, "Just cook with me." So, I did. But then I'd ask, "Mom, how much garlic did you just put in?" And she'd answer, "What, you didn't watch? You should be paying attention!" It took years of cooking with her before I finally got it.

2 (28-ounce) cans whole peeled tomatoes, undrained

3 tablespoons olive oil

½ small onion, minced

3 cloves garlic, minced

2 (28-ounce) cans tomato sauce

2 tablespoons minced fresh oregano

2 teaspoons salt

2 teaspoons sugar

Red pepper flakes to taste (optional)

3 tablespoons thinly sliced fresh basil

✳ In a large bowl, place the tomatoes with their liquid. (Get ready to get a bit messy!) Cut each tomato in half and remove the seeds with your fingers. Once that's done, squeeze and mash the tomatoes with your hands, letting them slip between your fingers until they become small chunks. (Like I said, this is a bit messy, but it's the old-school way and I don't like to mess with perfection.)

✳ In a 5- to 6-quart soup pot over medium heat, combine olive oil, onion, and garlic; sauté until onion is tender. Then, add the crushed tomatoes and the sauce. Increase heat to medium-high and heat the sauce until it comes to a boil, stirring frequently to prevent the bottom from scorching.

✳ Add the oregano, salt, sugar, and red pepper flakes, if desired. Reduce heat to low and simmer 1 hour, uncovered or until the sauce begins to thicken, stirring frequently. Stir in the basil. Remove from heat, and use as desired. (This sauce is so versatile; it can be used in any recipe that calls for spaghetti or marinara sauce.)

Chef Tony's Tip: A really good marinara sauce starts with really good tomatoes. I like to use whole tomatoes that are peeled, canned, and imported from Italy. I find that imported Italian tomatoes are meatier and more flavorful.

asian-inspired ramen bowls

Serves 4

My parents put me in martial arts classes as a kid because I was bullied. At 18, my teacher and my second dad, Sensei Tony Zuzio, took me under his wing and taught me for 25 years. Back in those days, part of the training involved understanding the culture of martial arts, which included food. Over the years, I've grown to love everything about Asian culture. Although my kicks are not as high as they used to be, I still hold a 5th degree black belt, which I am very proud of.

½ pound firm tofu, cut into 1-inch pieces

2 tablespoons cornstarch

¼ teaspoon salt

¼ teaspoon black pepper

1 tablespoon vegetable oil

2 teaspoons sesame oil

3 cloves garlic, minced

2 teaspoons minced fresh ginger

4 cups vegetable or miso broth

3 tablespoons soy sauce

1 cup sliced fresh mushrooms

2 (3-ounce) packages ramen noodles (seasoning packets discarded)

2 medium-soft-boiled eggs, cut in half (see Tip)

¼ cup thinly shredded carrots

1 scallion, sliced

¼ cup thinly sliced red bell pepper

✳ Place the tofu on paper towels and lightly pat to absorb excess liquid. In a medium bowl, combine the cornstarch, salt, and pepper; mix well. Add tofu; toss gently until evenly coated. In a large skillet over medium heat, heat vegetable oil until hot. Add tofu and sauté for 4 to 5 minutes or until golden, turning occasionally. Set aside.

✳ Meanwhile, in a soup pot over medium heat, heat sesame oil until hot. Add the garlic and ginger and cook 2 minutes. Add broth and soy sauce; bring to a boil. Stir in mushrooms and noodles, reduce heat to low, and simmer 5 to for 6 minutes or until the noodles are tender.

✳ Divide noodles evenly into soup bowls, add the broth mixture, and top with tofu, half an egg, the carrots, scallions, and bell pepper slices. Serve immediately with a soup spoon and chopsticks to make this as authentic as can be.

Chef Tony's Tip: To make perfect, medium-soft-boiled eggs for this, fill a saucepan with enough water to cover the eggs and bring to a boil over medium-high heat. Cover the saucepan, remove from heat, and let sit 8 minutes. Drain the eggs and cover with ice. Let sit for 5 minutes, then peel. They should be a bit firmer than traditional soft-boiled eggs.

Pasta & More

italian meat stromboli

Serves 6-8

A stromboli is basically a sandwich, wrapped up in pizza dough. It's loaded with lots of different meats and cheeses, and everyone makes it a little different. You'll see these on the menu of pizza restaurants everywhere, but they're so easy to make, I prefer to do it myself. I serve this with a side of marinara sauce for dipping, because everything tastes better with marinara sauce! (By the way, this is one of my family's Christmas traditions.)

1 (1 pound) fresh pizza dough (see Tip)

Flour for dusting

10 slices provolone cheese

⅓ pound sliced deli ham

⅓ pound sliced deli salami

⅓ pound sliced deli pepperoni

⅓ pound sliced deli capocollo

10 slices mozzarella cheese

1 tablespoon olive oil

1 tablespoon shredded Parmesan cheese

✳ Preheat oven to 400 degrees F. Coat a baking sheet with cooking spray.

✳ On a flat surface, roll out the dough into a 12- x 14-inch rectangle. (You'll want to lightly dust the counter and your rolling pin with a bit of flour to prevent them from sticking.) Layer the dough with slices of provolone cheese, topped with ham, salami, pepperoni, capocollo, and mozzarella cheese.

✳ Starting with the long end of the dough, roll up jelly roll-style and place it on the baking sheet, seam-side down. Brush with olive oil and sprinkle with Parmesan cheese.

✳ Bake for 20 to 25 minutes or until golden. Let sit 5 minutes, then slice, and serve.

Chef Tony's Tip: You don't have to make your own pizza dough from scratch. You can buy it at your favorite pizza shop or at the bakery at your local supermarket. Just ask for a ball of fresh pizza dough.

thin 'n' crispy veggie pizza

Serves 4-6

I think I've mentioned it a few times in this book already, but pizza is a HUGE thing in our house. My mom made pizza all the time when we were kids and I make pizza all the time now as an adult. It's easy, everyone loves it, and there are so many different ways to make it your own. For a "Meatless Monday" kind of pizza, try this version with lots of veggies on top.

2 tablespoons plus 1 teaspoon vegetable oil, divided

1 large red onion, thinly sliced

1 (1 pound) fresh pizza dough (from bakery)

½ cup pizza sauce

1 cup shredded mozzarella cheese

½ cup roasted red pepper strips

¼ cup sliced black olives

½ cup quartered artichoke hearts

½ cup sliced cremini mushrooms (Also called baby bellas, but almost any mushroom will work.)

✴ Preheat oven to 425 degrees F. Lightly brush a 14-inch round pizza pan with 1 teaspoon oil.

✴ In a large skillet over medium heat, heat remaining 2 tablespoons oil until hot; cook the onion for 15 to 20 minutes or until caramelized, stirring occasionally.

✴ Roll out dough to cover the bottom of the pizza pan. (I like a thinner crust for this, so roll it out nice and thin.) Spread the sauce evenly over dough (almost to the edge) and sprinkle with mozzarella cheese. Evenly top the cheese with the caramelized onions, then the pepper strips, black olives, artichoke hearts, and mushrooms.

✴ Bake for 15 to 18 minutes or until crust is crisp around the edges and the bottom is golden. Cut into slices and serve.

Chef Tony's Tip: If you have a pizza stone, this is a good time to dig it out. If you do, you need to preheat the stone in your oven and once your pizza is assembled, sprinkle the stone with cornmeal before sliding the pizza onto it to cook. This will ensure you get a nice golden crust like you get in a pizzeria.

"My Papa Frank was a produce man, which means that my family was blessed to have lots of fresh fruits and vegetables on the table when we were growing up."

great
go-alongs

zucchini & tomato casserole

Serves 6-8

One of my favorite summer pastimes is visiting farmer's markets and roadside produce stands. (This might have something to do with being the son of a produce guy...) I like to buy whatever looks the freshest, then take it home and whip up something with it. Zucchini and tomatoes are two great summer finds that I use to make this inspiring side dish casserole.

2 pounds zucchini

3 tablespoons olive oil, divided

½ teaspoon salt

¼ teaspoon black pepper

4 cloves garlic, minced

1 cup grape tomatoes, cut in half

¼ cup chopped fresh basil, plus extra for garnish

1 cup shredded Italian cheese blend, divided

½ cup Italian panko bread crumbs

✺ Preheat oven to 350 degrees F. Coat an 8-inch square baking dish with cooking spray. Cut the zucchini in half lengthwise, and then slice each half into ½-inch pieces. (This should give you about 7 cups.)

✺ In a large skillet over medium-high heat, heat 2 tablespoons oil. Add the zucchini, salt, and pepper, and cook 7 to 10 minutes or until tender, stirring frequently. Stir in garlic and cook 1 more minute; remove from heat.

✺ Add the tomatoes and ¼ cup basil to the zucchini mixture, stirring to combine. Spoon into the baking dish and top with ¾ cup of the cheese blend.

✺ In a small bowl, mix the bread crumbs, the remaining ¼ cup cheese and the remaining 1 tablespoon oil. Sprinkle this on top of the shredded cheese layer and bake for 30 to 35 minutes or until the veggies are heated through and the topping is golden. Top with additional chopped fresh basil just before serving.

Chef Tony's Tip: You can change this up by using a different cheese blend every time (Italian one day, Mexican another...you get the idea!).

crispy cabbage steaks

Serves 5-6

I've been cooking for a long time, but that doesn't mean I know every single thing there is to know. (That would be boring!) In fact, I love it when I get to learn something new in the kitchen. Just recently, a friend shared the idea of cooking cabbage "steaks" and I decided to give it a try. It may seem basic, but the results are so crispy and delicious, you've just got to try it.

1 head cabbage, dark outer leaves discarded

3 tablespoons olive oil

½ teaspoon onion powder

1 teaspoon kosher salt

½ teaspoon black pepper

✳ Preheat oven to 425 degrees F.

✳ Trim the core of the cabbage slightly so that the cabbage has a flat surface to sit on. (This will keep it from rolling around when you cut it.) Then with the core side down, cut into ½-inch "steaks." (Be careful, the cabbage is firm and you don't want the knife to slip!)

✳ In a small bowl, combine the oil, onion powder, salt, and pepper; mix well. Brush both sides of each cabbage "steak" with the oil mixture and place on a rimmed baking sheet.

✳ Roast for 25 to 30 minutes or until fork-tender and edges are crispy. At this point, if you like crispier edges, turn your oven to broil and broil until cabbage is to your liking.

Chef Tony's Tip: This same recipe can be made with cauliflower in place of the cabbage. However, you will need to add about 15 more minutes to the cooking time to ensure your cauliflower "steaks" are fork-tender.

lemony roasted broccoli

Serves 2-3

Make a broccoli lover out of anyone with this recipe for crispy, lemony, roasted broccoli. My kids and grandkids are pretty adventurous eaters, so I've never had much trouble getting them to eat their veggies, but if you've got picky eaters in your house, get them to try eating their broccoli this way. You won't have any problems the next time you add this to your dinner menu!

1 tablespoon olive oil

¼ teaspoon salt

¼ teaspoon black pepper

3 cups broccoli florets

2 teaspoons lemon juice

1 tablespoon grated Parmesan cheese

✺ Preheat oven to 400 degrees F.

✺ In a medium bowl, combine oil, salt, and pepper. Add the broccoli and toss until evenly coated. Place on a rimmed baking sheet.

✺ Roast 20 to 25 minutes or until the edges of the florets get super crispy and begin to char. (I suggest turning the florets halfway through the roasting time, so that they cook evenly.) If you like your veggies really crispy, add a few more minutes to the cooking time.

✺ Drizzle the broccoli with lemon juice, sprinkle with Parmesan cheese, and serve.

classic creamed spinach

Serves 4-5

Creamed spinach and I go way back. The first time I had it was in one of New York City's automats. (An automat was like a fast food restaurant where the food was kept inside vending machines.) I was just a kid then. When I got older, I got to try it at some fancy steakhouses. Finally, I decided to start making it myself. This recipe is a classic one that delivers some seriously good results.

1 tablespoon butter

2 (9-ounce) packages frozen chopped spinach, thawed and squeezed dry

1 cup heavy cream

1 cup sour cream

1 teaspoon onion powder

1 teaspoon ground nutmeg

½ teaspoon salt

½ teaspoon black pepper

✳ In a medium saucepan over medium heat, melt the butter; add spinach and stir until heated through.

✳ Add the remaining ingredients to the spinach and cook for 4 to 5 minutes or until heated through, stirring occasionally. Serve immediately.

Chef Tony's Tip: You can make this recipe ahead of time. Just place the cooked mixture in a 2-quart casserole dish and bake it covered, at 350 degrees for about 20 minutes or until it's bubbling hot.

creamy corn with crumbled bacon

Serves 6-8

Looking for the perfect side dish to team up with your holiday ham or that special occasion roast? I've got you covered! This is one that I love to make when I've got the whole family coming over. Everyone loves the combination of creamy corn with bits of bacon in every bite. And there's the crispy onion topping too! When you make this side dish, you'll be delivering lots of mouthwatering goodness.

1 teaspoon olive oil

½ cup chopped onion

2 tablespoons butter, softened

6 ounces cream cheese, softened, (see Tip)

1 (15-¼-ounce) can cream-style corn

1 (15-¼-ounce) can whole kernel corn, drained

⅓ cup cooked and crumbled bacon

1 cup French-fried onions

❋ Preheat oven to 350 degrees F. Coat an 8-inch square baking dish or 1-½ quart baking dish with cooking spray.

❋ In a small skillet over medium heat, heat oil until hot; sauté the onion 3 to 5 minutes or until tender.

❋ In a large bowl, combine the butter and cream cheese. Stir in both cans of corn, the sautéed onions, and bacon. Pour into baking dish and bake for 15 minutes.

❋ Remove from oven, sprinkle the top with French-fried onions, and bake an additional 15 to 20 minutes or until the center is hot and the top is golden.

Chef Tony's Tip: You don't need a scale to measure out 6 ounces of cream cheese. Simply cut a quarter off of an 8-ounce block. You can use the remaining 2 ounces to schmear on your bagels the next morning!

Great Go-Alongs

bacon & onion brussels sprouts

Serves 4-6

Normally when I walk into a grocery store, I don't have a plan. I have no clue what I'm going to eat. Instead, I look for inspiration. Sometimes I start in the meat department, other times I go to the produce section. Here's a recipe I came up with during one of my inspirational visits. It features crispy bacon (the way I like it) and sautéed onions tossed with roasted Brussels sprouts. It's joy on a plate!

¼ cup olive oil

½ teaspoon garlic powder

¼ teaspoon onion powder

½ teaspoon salt

¼ teaspoon black pepper

1 pound Brussels sprouts, trimmed and cut in half

4 slices bacon

½ cup chopped onion

✳ Preheat oven to 425 degrees F.

✳ In a large bowl, combine oil, garlic powder, onion powder, salt, and pepper. Add the Brussels sprouts and toss gently until evenly coated. Place on a rimmed baking sheet.

✳ Roast 25 to 30 minutes or until tender and the edges are crispy, turning once halfway through cooking.

✳ Meanwhile, in a large skillet over medium-high heat, cook the bacon for 8 to 10 minutes or until crispy, turning once halfway through. Remove to a paper towel-lined plate, reserving the bacon drippings in the skillet. Let bacon cool, then crumble.

✳ Place the onion in the skillet with bacon drippings and cook over medium heat for 5 to 7 minutes or until tender. In a large bowl, toss the roasted Brussel sprouts with the onion and sprinkle with bacon. Serve immediately.

Great Go-Alongs

cranberry pecan stuffing

Serves 6-8

In my kitchen, stuffing is like a blank canvas that you can add this or that to, to create your own masterpiece. So beyond making this the way I suggest to, feel free to change it up by adding chopped fresh apples, mandarin orange segments, or even cooked chicken gizzards (like my mom did). This is a great recipe to experiment with your foodie skills!

1 stick butter

1 cup chopped onion

1 cup chopped celery

3 cups chicken broth

1 cup dried cranberries

½ cup chopped pecans

1 (14-ounce) package herb-seasoned stuffing

❈ Preheat oven to 350 degrees F. Spray a 3-quart casserole dish with cooking spray.

❈ In a large saucepan or soup pot over medium-high heat, melt the butter. Add the onion and celery and cook for 6 to 8 minutes or until tender. Add the broth and continue cooking until hot. Add the cranberries, pecans, and stuffing; gently stir until well combined.

❈ Spoon into the casserole dish and bake covered, for 30 minutes. Uncover and bake an additional 15 minutes or until heated through and the top begins to turn golden brown.

pop's rice stuffing

Serves 8-10

Even though mom did most of the cooking growing up, my pop was the king when it came to stuffing. His stuffing was far from ordinary. It was an Italian-style stuffing that was loaded with sausage and veggies, and held together by rice. We used it to stuff turkey, pork chops, chicken, peppers...you name it. My family is addicted to this stuffing, and I bet you'll be too!

1 pound sweet Italian sausage, casings removed (about 4 sausages)

2 tablespoons butter

2 tablespoons olive oil

8 ounces mushrooms, cut into quarters

1 cup finely diced celery

1 cup finely diced sweet onion

2 cups cooked long grain rice

2 tablespoons Italian seasoning

1 cup grated Romano cheese, divided

½ cup chopped fresh parsley

¼ teaspoon salt

½ teaspoon black pepper

✺ Preheat oven to 350 degrees F. Coat a 2-quart baking dish with cooking spray.

✺ In a large skillet over medium-high heat, sauté the sausage until no pink remains, breaking it up into small pieces; drain off excess liquid. Remove sausage to a large bowl and set aside.

✺ In the same skillet over medium heat, melt butter and heat oil until hot. Add the mushrooms, celery, and onion; sauté for 5 minutes or until onion is tender. Add to the bowl of sausage.

✺ In the same bowl, add the cooked rice, Italian seasoning, ¾ cup Romano cheese, the parsley, salt, and pepper; mix well.

✺ Pour mixture into the baking dish, cover with aluminum foil, and bake for 25 minutes. Remove foil, sprinkle the remaining ¼ cup Romano cheese on top, and bake an additional 10 minutes or until the center is hot and the cheese is golden.

Chef Tony's Tip: No Romano cheese? No problem. You can use Parmesan or a similar, grated, Italian hard cheese.

garlic escarole with toasted garbanzos

Serves 6-8

I'm a greens man. I love everything from everyday spinach and broccoli rabe to the more exotic greens like dandelion and snow pea leaves. Escarole is another favorite too – I use it a lot to make soups and salads. If you love greens like I do, then you'll really enjoy this flavor-packed escarole side dish. It's garlicky, it's got a bit of a crunch (from the pan-toasted garbanzo beans), and it really highlights the escarole. Trust me, you don't want to skip this!

2 large bunches escarole

¼ cup olive oil

5 cloves garlic, thinly sliced

1 (7.75-ounce) can garbanzo beans, drained well

½ teaspoon salt

¼ teaspoon black pepper

❊ Remove and discard the outer leaves from escarole and trim off root end. Tear the leaves into large pieces and wash them well in cold water.

❊ Place the escarole in a soup pot and completely cover with water. Bring to a boil over high heat and cook for about 3 minutes or just until tender. Remove from heat, drain well, and pat dry.

❊ In a large skillet over medium heat, heat oil until hot. Add the garlic and garbanzo beans and sauté for 3 to 5 minutes or until both are lightly toasted. Add escarole, salt, and pepper; toss well and heat for 3 to 5 minutes or until hot.

Chef Tony's Tip: You'll know the garbanzo beans are toasted just right when the skins on them start to crackle and blister.

extra-creamy hash browns

Serves 8-10

Serve up an extra side of comfort with my recipe for extra-creamy hash browns. With just five ingredients, it doesn't get any easier than this. You don't even need to shred the potatoes, because I make this with frozen, shredded, hash browns. Grab a big serving spoon, because everyone is going to want a heaping spoonful of these!

2 cups (8 ounces) shredded cheddar cheese

1 (16-ounce) container sour cream

2 (10-¾-ounce) cans condensed potato soup

3 scallions sliced

1 (30-ounce) package frozen shredded hash browns, thawed

❈ Preheat oven to 375 degrees F. Coat a 9- x 13-inch baking dish with cooking spray.

❈ In a large bowl, combine the cheddar cheese, sour cream, potato soup, and scallions; mix well. Gently fold in the hash browns and toss to coat.

❈ Pour into the prepared baking dish. With a fork, fluff up the potatoes so that the tips will get crispy as this bakes.

❈ Bake for 50 to 60 minutes or until heated through and the top is crispy. Serve piping hot.

Chef Tony's Tip: You can also make this using frozen potato tots. It'll change the texture a bit, but the taste will be the same!

two-mushroom risotto

Serves 4-6

When company comes a-calling, it's good to know you've got luxurious recipes like this one on hand. Here, you've got creamy risotto made with two varieties of mushrooms (to add some complex textures and flavors). This one is good enough to be served as a main dish too – just add some cooked chicken or shrimp and you've got yourself a meal that's fit for a king!

3 cups chicken broth

5 tablespoons butter, divided

1 (8-ounce) package white mushrooms, sliced

1 (8-ounce) package cremini mushrooms, sliced

½ cup finely chopped onion

1 cup uncooked Arborio rice

1 teaspoon minced garlic

⅓ cup white wine

¼ cup grated Parmesan cheese

1 tablespoon chopped fresh parsley

¼ teaspoon black pepper

✳ In a medium saucepan over medium heat, bring the chicken broth to a simmer; do not let boil. Keep warm over low heat.

✳ Meanwhile, in a large saucepan over medium-high heat, melt 4 tablespoons of butter. Add both types mushrooms and the onion, and sauté 4 to 5 minutes or until tender. Stir in the rice, garlic, and wine; cook until wine is absorbed. Add 1 cup hot broth, stirring constantly until liquid is nearly absorbed. Repeat process, adding remaining broth 1 cup at a time, and stirring constantly until each addition of the broth is absorbed before adding the next cup. (This will take about 15 minutes. Don't rush this step – it's what makes the risotto really good!)

✳ Remove from heat. Stir in remaining 1 tablespoon butter, the cheese, parsley, and pepper. Serve immediately. (If you let this sit, you might have to add a little more broth to keep it nice and creamy.)

italian-style poutine

Serves 6-8

Traditionally, poutine is made by sprinkling cheese curds on top of crispy french fries and drizzling gravy over everything. Sounds pretty great, right? Well, I wanted to put my own twist on this Canadian favorite, so for my version I replaced the curds with small balls of fresh mozzarella. As it turns out, my way is pretty great too. I can't wait to hear what you foodies think about this!

1 (32-ounce) package frozen crinkle-cut french fries

½ stick butter

¼ cup all-purpose flour

1-¾ cups beef broth

¼ teaspoon salt

¼ teaspoon black pepper

1 teaspoon browning and seasoning sauce

8 ounces small fresh mozzarella balls, drained

✳ Bake french fries according to package directions.

✳ Meanwhile, in a medium saucepan over medium heat, melt the butter. Add the flour and whisk until smooth and mixture begins to turn golden. Slowly whisk in the broth, salt, and pepper, and continue stirring until the mixture comes to a boil and has thickened. Stir in the browning and seasoning sauce.

✳ Place french fries on a platter or in a shallow casserole dish, top with the mozzarella balls, and drizzle with gravy. Serve immediately.

Chef Tony's Tip: If you have extra gravy, serve it in a gravy boat and pour it on as you eat your way to the bottom of the dish. There's no such thing as too much gravy!

mashed potato croquettes

Serves 6-8

Tired of serving mashed potatoes the same old way as always? Keep your family on their toes by serving them this way instead. On the outside, these croquettes are crispy and golden, while on the inside they're creamy and comforting. Serve these alongside your family's favorite greens and watch their faces light up with joy!

2 cups cold mashed potatoes (leftover or refrigerated store-bought)

2 egg yolks

½ cup grated Parmesan cheese

1 tablespoon all-purpose flour

2 tablespoons chopped fresh chives

2 eggs

¾ cups bread crumbs

1 cup vegetable oil

❋ In a large bowl, combine the mashed potatoes, egg yolks, Parmesan cheese, flour, and chives. Form the mixture into about 20 (2-inch) log-shaped croquettes and chill for 20 minutes.

❋ Meanwhile in a shallow bowl, beat the eggs. In another shallow bowl, place the bread crumbs.

❋ In a medium deep skillet over medium heat, heat oil until hot, but not smoking. (You'll know the oil is at the right temperature when you add a pinch of bread crumbs to the oil and it bubbles immediately. It should be at about 325 degrees.)

❋ Dip the chilled croquettes in egg, then roll in bread crumbs, making sure that croquettes are evenly covered. Working in batches, fry croquettes for 3 to 4 minutes, or until golden brown and crisp, turning often. Drain on paper towels and serve warm.

Chef Tony's Tip: You can make these ahead of time. When you're ready to serve them, just place them on a baking sheet and warm them up in a 300-degree oven for about 10 minutes.

simple
picnic coleslaw

Serves 8-10

Coleslaw just screams summer. It's the ultimate picnic side dish, the best friend of fried chicken, and the must-have on every barbecue plate. If you've been relying on prepared coleslaws your whole life, one taste of this will make you reconsider. You get so much flavor out of my slaw, thanks to the addition of colorful veggies and a ridiculously good homemade dressing. Your summer is going to get a whole lot brighter.

1 head green cabbage, shredded

2 carrots, peeled and shredded

½ red bell pepper, chopped

2 tablespoons diced red onion

1 cup mayonnaise

2 tablespoons white vinegar

3 tablespoons sugar

½ teaspoon salt

¼ tablespoon white pepper

✳ In a large bowl, combine the cabbage, carrots, bell pepper, and onion; mix well and set aside.

✳ In a small bowl, combine the remaining ingredients; mix well. Pour over the cabbage mixture; toss to coat well. Cover and chill for at least 1 hour or until ready to serve.

Chef Tony's Tip: To make shredding the cabbage and carrots really easy, use a mandoline. If you're looking for the easiest shortcut, you could also use two (10-ounce) packages of shredded cabbage and carrots, instead of shredding them yourself.

old world potato salad

Serves 6-8

I've made potato salad many different ways over the years, so you can imagine how hard it was for me to choose just one to share with you guys in this cookbook. Since most people tend to think of potato salad as served cold, I decided to go with this Old World version that's served warm and has a unique dressing to it. (Plus, I sort of love that it has bacon in it too...)

4 pounds potatoes, peeled and thinly sliced

8 slices bacon

¼ cup vegetable oil

½ cup finely chopped onion

½ cup white vinegar

¼ cup water

⅓ cup sugar

1 teaspoon salt

3 tablespoons finely chopped fresh parsley

- In a large pot of boiling water, cook potatoes for 10 to 15 minutes or until fork tender. Drain carefully, place in a large bowl, and set aside.
- Meanwhile, in a large skillet over medium heat, cook the bacon until browned and crisp, turning as needed. Remove to a paper towel-lined plate, reserving the bacon drippings in the skillet. Let bacon cool, then crumble.
- In the same skillet, add the oil and onion and cook for 4 to 5 minutes or until onion is tender. Stir in the vinegar, water, sugar and salt; bring to a boil. Gently stir in the potatoes and parsley.
- Add half of the bacon to the potato mixture and heat until warmed through, stirring occasionally. Remove to a serving dish, sprinkle the remaining bacon over top, and serve warm.

honey butter glazed sweet potatoes

Serves 5-6

Vivian and I love our sweet potatoes. They're a regular side dish in our weekly routine, prepared one way or another. And when it comes to special occasions, like Thanksgiving, you can bet they're on the menu too. This way of making them is good no matter when you decide to do it. The honey butter glaze complements the sweet potatoes so perfectly, it's basically a match made in kitchen heaven.

5 tablespoons butter, melted

3 tablespoons honey

1 teaspoon vanilla extract

1 teaspoon ground cinnamon

3 pounds sweet potatoes, peeled and cut into 1-inch pieces

Sea salt for sprinkling

✳ Preheat oven to 350 degrees F. Coat a rimmed baking sheet with cooking spray.

✳ In a large bowl, whisk together the butter, honey, vanilla, and cinnamon. Add the sweet potatoes and toss well to coat evenly.

✳ Spread the coated potatoes in an even layer on the baking sheet. Bake for 45 to 50 minutes or until tender, stirring twice during baking. Place in a serving bowl and drizzle with the remaining honey mixture from pan. Sprinkle with sea salt and serve immediately.

Chef Tony's Tip: To make cleanup a breeze, before coating the pan with cooking spray, line it with aluminum foil. Then go ahead and spray it. This will allow you to toss out the sticky mess rather than soaking the pan and scrubbing off the honey that's stuck to it.

restaurant-style garlic knots

Makes 12

It's hard to resist a garlic roll, especially when you go to a restaurant and they bring them out stacked high in a little basket, just dripping with garlic and butter. (Oh boy, my mouth is watering!) If you want to live out your garlic roll dreams at home, now you can. Just make sure everyone gets one, so that you're not alone with your not-so-fresh-but-totally-worth-it breath!

½ stick butter

4 cloves garlic, minced

2 tablespoons chopped fresh parsley

¼ teaspoon salt

1 (13.8-ounce) package refrigerated classic pizza dough

✳ Preheat oven to 400 degrees F.

✳ In a small saucepan over low heat, melt the butter. Stir in the garlic, parsley, and salt and heat for 2 minutes; set aside.

✳ Unroll the pizza dough on a cutting board and cut into 12 (1-inch-wide) strips. "Tie" each strip of dough into a knot, tucking the ends under the knot. Place on a rimmed baking sheet. Brush half the garlic-butter mixture over the rolls.

✳ Bake for 12 to 14 minutes or until golden. Right before serving, brush the rolls with remaining garlic-butter and serve. (You may need to warm the butter mixture up in the microwave for a few seconds so that it will soak into every nook and cranny.)

Chef Tony's Tip: These would go great served with my Old World Pasta Bolognese (page 136) or My Childhood Lasagna (page 138). Also, I love to sprinkle on some grated Parmesan cheese after the second brushing of garlic butter... mmmm!

"OK, I have to admit... I've got a real sweet tooth. I like everything from pies and cakes, to cookies, brownies, and mousse!"

to-die-for desserts

celebration cannoli cake

Serves 12-14

This recipe has been a mainstay at many family celebrations, and now you can make it the centerpiece of yours. It's great for birthdays, holidays, anniversaries...you name it! Not only does it look spectacular, but the taste is incredible too. From the homemade cannoli filling to the fluffy whipped cream frosting, there's more than one reason to celebrate this cake!

Cannoli Filling

1-½ cups ricotta cheese

2 (8-ounce) containers mascarpone cheese

⅓ cup powdered sugar

½ teaspoon orange extract

¾ cup mini chocolate chips

⅛ teaspoon ground cinnamon

1 package white cake mix, baked according to package directions for 2 (8-inch) cakes, cooled

¼ cup refrigerated strawberry glaze or pie filling

1 cup fresh strawberries, thinly sliced

1 (3-ounce) package mini cannoli shells

Whipped Cream Frosting

2 cups heavy cream

2 tablespoons powdered sugar

3 teaspoons instant vanilla pudding mix

½ teaspoon vanilla extract

✹ To make Cannoli Filling, in a large bowl, combine ricotta cheese, mascarpone cheese, ⅓ cup powdered sugar, and the orange extract; stir gently just until combined. Stir in chocolate chips and cinnamon. Cover and refrigerate 1 hour or until the mixture is firm.

✹ Meanwhile, slice each cake in half horizontally. Place one cake layer on a platter and spread with ½ cup cannoli filling. Place second cake layer on top and spread with strawberry glaze and top with sliced strawberries. Place third cake layer on top of strawberries and spread with ½ cup cannoli filling. Place fourth cake layer on top and place in the refrigerator.

✹ Using a pastry bag or plastic storage bag with one corner snipped, fill cannoli shells with remaining cannoli filling. Cover, and place in the refrigerator.

✹ To make Whipped Cream Frosting, in a large bowl, beat heavy cream 1 minute. Add 2 tablespoons powdered sugar, the instant vanilla pudding mix, and vanilla; continue beating 2 to 4 minutes or until stiff peaks form. Frost top and sides of cake with frosting. Refrigerate the cake at least 2 hours or until ready to serve. Just before serving, decorate the cake with cannoli as shown.

s'mores poke cake

Serves 12-15

Good news - you don't have to go camping to enjoy s'mores! The only time I ever tried to take my family on a camping trip it didn't end so well for me. (I had a work emergency, but the family had a blast.) So nowadays, I make my family some of their camping favorites (like s'mores) right at home. This easy-to-make cake features the classic s'mores trio of marshmallows, chocolate, and graham crackers, and it's 100% shareable.

1 package chocolate cake mix, baked according to package directions for a 9- x 13-inch baking dish, cooled

1 (14-ounce) container hot fudge ice cream topping

Marshmallow Frosting

2 sticks butter, softened

1 cup marshmallow crème

1 teaspoon vanilla extract

4 cups powdered sugar

4 graham crackers, cut in quarters

½ cup mini marshmallows

1 (1.55-ounce) chocolate candy bar, grated

✺ Using the end of a wooden spoon, poke holes about 1-inch apart all over top of cake. (If the cake starts to stick to the wooden spoon, just wipe it clean with a wet paper towel.)

✺ Heat hot fudge in the microwave for 30 to 60 seconds or until pourable. Slowly pour the hot fudge into the holes and spread evenly over top of cake. Refrigerate 1 hour or until the fudge sets up.

✺ Meanwhile to make Marshmallow Frosting, in a large bowl using an electric mixer, beat butter, marshmallow crème, and vanilla until creamy. Slowly add powdered sugar, and beat until smooth. Frost top of cake and garnish with graham crackers, mini marshmallows, and grated chocolate, as shown.

keep-it-simple new york cheesecake

Serves 14-16

It's the truth - I like my cheesecake plain. Hold the berries. Hold the fluff. Hold the everything. You see, I was raised on Junior's cheesecakes in New York. (I remember walking down DeKalb Avenue with my mom to buy them.) And Junior's cheesecakes are so good, you don't need to top them or serve them with anything else, in my opinion. This cheesecake is like that. You COULD serve it with your favorite toppings, but you certainly don't have to.

1-½ cups graham cracker crumbs

2 tablespoons plus 1 cup sugar, divided

1 teaspoon ground cinnamon

5 tablespoons butter, melted

3 (8-ounce) packages cream cheese, softened

1 cup sour cream

4 eggs

1 teaspoon vanilla extract

✳ Preheat oven to 450 degrees F. Coat a 9-inch springform pan with cooking spray; set aside.

✳ In a medium bowl, combine graham cracker crumbs, 2 tablespoons sugar, and the cinnamon; mix well. Add the butter and mix until the crumbs are thoroughly coated. Pour the crumb mixture into the pan and using your fingertips, press down until the crumbs evenly cover the bottom of the pan.

✳ In a large bowl using an electric mixer on medium speed, beat cream cheese, sour cream, remaining 1 cup sugar, the eggs, and vanilla until thoroughly combined and mixture is smooth. Pour the mixture into the springform pan and place the pan on a baking sheet. (If you gently shake the pan, it will level out the batter and get rid of any air bubbles in it.) Bake 15 minutes, then lower the oven temperature to 200 degrees.

✳ Bake about 1 hour or until the center of the cheesecake is slightly wiggly. Turn the oven off, crack the door open, and let the cheesecake slowly cool down in the oven for about 1 hour. Then remove from oven and when cooled completely at room temperature, run a thin knife around the edge of the cheesecake. Refrigerate overnight or until ready to serve.

go-to
carrot cake

Serves 12-15

I love a good carrot cake! If you're looking for an easy "go-to" recipe that'll satisfy your cravings, then this is it. Simple, moist, and sweet, this carrot cake always puts a smile on my face (and I'm sure it'll put one on your face too!). I'm not saying you have to make it right now, but...why not?

2 cups all-purpose flour

2 teaspoons baking soda

½ teaspoon salt

2 teaspoons ground cinnamon

3 eggs

¾ cup buttermilk

¾ cup vegetable oil

2 cups granulated sugar

2 teaspoons vanilla extract

1 (8-ounce) can crushed pineapple, drained

¾ cup chopped walnuts

3 cups shredded carrots

Cream Cheese Frosting

1 (8-ounce) package cream cheese, softened

3 tablespoons butter, softened

1 teaspoon vanilla extract

1 cup powdered sugar

✸ Preheat oven to 350 degrees F. Coat a 9- x 13-inch baking dish with cooking spray; set aside.

✸ In a medium bowl, combine flour, baking soda, salt, and cinnamon; mix well and set aside.

✸ In a large bowl using an electric mixer on low speed, beat eggs, buttermilk, oil, granulated sugar, and 2 teaspoons vanilla. Add the pineapple, walnuts, and the carrots; mix well. Beat in the flour mixture until well combined, then pour into the baking dish.

✸ Bake 35 to 40 minutes or until a toothpick inserted in center comes out clean; let cool.

✸ Meanwhile, in a medium bowl, combine Cream Cheese Frosting ingredients, except powdered sugar. Slowly mix in the powdered sugar until smooth and creamy. Frost the cake, cut into squares, and serve.

Chef Tony's Tip: You can also use this recipe to make carrot cake cupcakes! Just pour the batter into cupcake pans with liners and bake for about 15 to 18 minutes.

5-star chocolate mousse cake

Serves 12-14

I make a really good chocolate mousse – it was passed down to me from my grandma. It's decadently rich and smooth, which is what makes it so irresistible. If you want to make something fancy for your family or to impress that someone special, then this is the dessert for you. It's like having a 5-star restaurant dessert at home.

3 cups finely crushed chocolate graham crackers

1 stick butter, melted

2 eggs

4 egg yolks

4 cups semisweet chocolate chips, divided

2 cups heavy cream

⅓ cup powdered sugar

12 fresh strawberries

1 teaspoon shortening

❀ In a medium bowl, combine the graham cracker crumbs and butter; mix well. Pour the crumb mixture into a 9-inch springform pan and using your fingertips, press the mixture into the bottom and up sides of the pan, creating a crust. Chill until ready to use.

❀ In a small bowl, beat eggs and egg yolks; set aside.

❀ In a soup pot over low heat, melt 3 cups of chocolate chips, stirring constantly. Slowly add the egg mixture, stirring quickly until well blended. Remove from heat; set aside to cool slightly.

❀ Meanwhile, in a medium bowl using an electric mixer on medium speed, whip heavy cream until soft peaks form. Add the powdered sugar and beat until stiff peaks form.

❀ Fold the whipped cream into the slightly cooled chocolate mixture until well blended. Spoon into crust, cover, and chill at least 6 hours or until firm.

❀ In a small microwave-safe bowl, combine remaining 1 cup of chocolate chips and the shortening. Microwave 60 to 90 seconds, stirring occasionally until smooth. Dip the strawberries halfway into the chocolate, and place on a wax paper-lined platter until the chocolate hardens. Garnish the cake with chocolate-covered strawberries.

sour cream pound cake

Serves 10-12

Mom was famous for her pound cakes. One of my favorites was her sour cream pound cake. The memory of it takes me back to those good ol' days. Unfortunately, her original recipe was lost in a couple of family disasters (a house fire and a house flood – can you believe it?!), but over the years I finally came up with a recipe that was just as good as hers. I even bake mine in a Bundt pan, just like she did.

2 sticks butter, softened

3 cups sugar

1 cup sour cream

6 eggs

3 cups all-purpose flour

¼ teaspoon baking soda

1 teaspoon vanilla extract

❋ Preheat oven to 325 degrees F. Generously coat a Bundt pan with cooking spray and dust with flour.

❋ In a large bowl using an electric mixer, cream together butter and sugar until light and fluffy. Blend in sour cream. Add eggs, one at a time, beating well after each addition. Combine flour and baking soda and gradually add to the batter. Mix well, then add vanilla. Pour batter evenly into pan.

❋ Bake 1-¼ to 1-½ hours, or until a toothpick comes out clean. Let the cake cool 30 minutes, then turn it out onto a serving plate and let cool completely.

Chef Tony's Tip: I like to serve this with some sliced strawberries and fresh whipped cream. You can also pan-sear some thicker slices in a skillet with a little butter on each side, for breakfast (my personal favorite!).

little italy layer cake

Serves 14-16

This cake brings me back to the Italian bakery on Avenue U, in the old neighborhood in Brooklyn. Whenever I'd look in the bakery case, this cake always seemed to call to me to bring it home. It's got layer after layer of moist white cake filled with buttery-rich pecans and sweet coconut flakes. Plus, between each layer, there's cream cheese frosting that brings it all together in the most delicious way.

1 package white cake mix

1-¼ cups buttermilk

3 large eggs

¼ cup vegetable oil

1 (3-½-ounce) can flaked coconut (see Tip)

1-⅔ cups chopped pecans, toasted, divided

3 tablespoons rum (optional)

2 (16-ounce) containers cream cheese frosting

✳ Preheat oven to 350 degrees F. Coat 3 (9-inch) round cake pans with cooking spray and dust with flour.

✳ In a large bowl using an electric mixer on medium speed, beat cake mix, buttermilk, eggs, and oil for 2 minutes. Stir in coconut and ⅔ cup pecans. Pour evenly into pans. Bake 15 to 17 minutes or until a toothpick inserted in center comes out clean.

✳ Cool in pans on wire racks for 10 minutes. Remove from pans and let cool completely on wire racks.

✳ Drizzle each cake layer with rum, if desired; let stand 10 minutes. Stir the frosting with the remaining 1 cup of chopped pecans. Place one cake (bottom-side up) on a serving platter and top it with ½ cup of the frosting. Top with another layer of cake (also, bottom-side up) and top it with another ½ cup of the frosting. Place the third cake (curved-side up) on top and frost the entire cake with the remaining frosting. Refrigerate for at least 2 hours before serving.

Chef Tony's Tip: By using canned flaked coconut you get bigger pieces in every bite. If you can't find it, regular shredded coconut will work. Also, toasting the pecans adds a richer flavor. To toast them, place them on a baking sheet and into a 350-degree oven for about 4 to 5 minutes. Just make sure you keep an eye on them, so that they don't burn.

white chocolate stuffed cupcakes

Makes 20

All of my kids love making and eating cupcakes (especially the stuffed kind). These are extra special, because the frosting is on top AND inside of each cupcake, which is a pretty sweet surprise. If you have to make a dessert for a wedding or an anniversary celebration, you should consider making these. Your guests will love their look and the surprise filling.

1 package devil's food cake mix

1 cup water

½ cup vegetable oil

3 eggs

2 teaspoons vanilla extract

White Chocolate Frosting

¾ cup white chocolate chips

¼ cup heavy cream

2 sticks butter, softened

5-½ cups powdered sugar

✳ Preheat oven to 350 degrees F. Line 20 cupcake cups with paper liners.

✳ In a large bowl using an electric mixer on medium speed, beat cake mix, water, oil, eggs, and vanilla until thoroughly combined. Evenly divide the batter into paper liners. Bake 15 to 18 minutes or until a toothpick comes out clean; let cool completely.

✳ Using an apple corer or paring knife, cut out the center of each cupcake, about ½-inch wide and 1-inch deep, making sure to leave the sides and bottom intact.

✳ To make White Chocolate Frosting, in a medium microwave-safe bowl, combine white chocolate chips and heavy cream. Microwave 60 to 75 seconds or until smooth, stirring occasionally; let cool slightly. In a large bowl using an electric mixer on medium speed, beat butter until creamy. Mix in the white chocolate mixture until thoroughly combined. Gradually beat in powdered sugar until frosting is light and fluffy.

✳ Using a plastic storage bag with one corner snipped or a pastry bag, pipe the filling evenly into the center of each cupcake. Pipe the remaining frosting on top. Keep refrigerated until ready to serve.

To-Die-For Desserts

chocolate almond crunch cake

Serves 10-12

I grew up eating this cake almost weekly. Mom loved to make it (and we all loved eating it!). I like it because the cake is really moist, but also light and spongy with a really nice sweetness to it. The homemade chocolate frosting along with the chopped almonds, adds the perfect finishing touches. You don't have to be elegant with this one, since no matter how you slice it, people are going to be all over it.

1 package yellow cake mix

1 cup milk

⅓ cup vegetable oil

3 eggs

1-½ teaspoons almond extract

⅓ cup chopped almonds

2 tablespoons almond liqueur or simple syrup

Chocolate Almond Frosting

1-½ sticks butter, softened

2 teaspoons almond extract

⅔ cup unsweetened cocoa powder

5 tablespoons milk

5 cups powdered sugar

¾ cup chopped almonds, divided

❋ Preheat oven to 350 degrees F. Coat the bottoms of 2 (9-inch) round cake pans with cooking spray. (In this case, don't spray the sides of the pan, or your cake won't rise properly while it bakes.)

❋ In a large bowl using an electric mixer, beat cake mix, 1 cup milk, the oil, eggs, and 1-½ teaspoons almond extract until thoroughly combined. Pour the batter evenly into the pans.

❋ Bake 20 to 25 minutes or until a toothpick inserted in center comes out clean. Let cool 10 minutes, then remove to wire racks to cool completely. While cooling, brush the tops of both cakes with almond liqueur or simple syrup.

❋ To make Chocolate Almond Frosting, in a large bowl using an electric mixer, beat butter and 2 teaspoons almond extract until creamy. Add cocoa powder and milk, beating until thoroughly combined. Slowly add powdered sugar, beating until smooth.

❋ Place first cake layer on a platter and frost top. Sprinkle with ¼ cup almonds. Place second cake layer on top, and frost top and sides. Sprinkle the top and sides with remaining ½ cup almonds.

Chef Tony's Tip: Brushing the cake with liqueur or even a little simple syrup is an easy way to add moisture to the cake before you begin frosting. I never skip this step!

italian bakery tiramisu

Serves 8-10

What kind of Italian would I be if I didn't include Italy's most popular dessert in my cookbook? This tiramisu is bakery quality and features layer after layer of rich, creamy goodness. Tiramisu means "pick me up" in Italian, and I can't think of a better name to fit this amazing dessert.

½ cup strong black coffee

¼ cup coffee-flavored liqueur

½ teaspoon vanilla extract

2 (8-ounce) containers mascarpone cheese

1 cup sugar

2 cups (1 pint) heavy cream

2 (3-ounce) packages ladyfingers (see Tip)

½ teaspoon unsweetened cocoa powder

✳ In a small bowl, combine coffee, liqueur, and vanilla; set aside.

✳ In a large bowl, beat the mascarpone cheese and sugar until smooth; set aside.

✳ In a medium bowl, whip the heavy cream until stiff peaks form. Fold 1-½ cups of whipped cream into mascarpone mixture until thoroughly combined; set aside remaining whipped cream.

✳ Line the bottom of an 8-inch square baking dish with ladyfingers. (It's okay if you have to overlap them a little bit for them to fit.) Spoon half of the coffee mixture evenly over the ladyfingers. Spoon half of the cheese mixture evenly over the ladyfingers. Layer with more ladyfingers and repeat with coffee mixture and cheese mixture.

✳ Spoon the remaining whipped cream over the top and sprinkle with cocoa powder. Cover and refrigerate for at least 3 hours before enjoying.

Chef Tony's Tip: You'll need the sponge-like ladyfingers for this recipe. Depending on what brand you buy, you might find yourself with a few extras to nibble on.

irresistible
double chocolate brownies

Serves 14-18

My kids are pretty smart. When they wanted something like a school trip or an iPad, they knew just how to bribe Daddy... with brownies! Ooey, gooey, and loaded up with lots of chopped walnuts. Those are the key things to making an irresistible brownie, and once you give these a try, I'm sure you'll agree.

3 sticks butter

3 cups sugar

5 eggs

2 teaspoons vanilla extract

1-¼ cups all-purpose flour

1-¼ cups unsweetened cocoa powder

1 teaspoon salt

1 cup chopped walnuts

1 cup semi-sweet chocolate chips

✳ Preheat oven to 350 degrees F. Coat a 9- x 13-inch baking dish with cooking spray.

✳ In a large saucepan over medium heat, melt butter. Stir in sugar until dissolved. Remove mixture from heat and let cool slightly. Beat in eggs, one at a time, mixing well after each addition. Stir in vanilla and set aside.

✳ In a medium bowl, stir together flour, cocoa powder, and salt. Add this to the butter mixture, mixing until combined. Stir in walnuts and chocolate chips. Spread the batter evenly in the baking dish.

✳ Bake 30 to 35 minutes or until a toothpick inserted in center comes out clean. Let cool completely before cutting and serving.

Chef Tony's Tip: Although I love the combo of the walnuts and chocolate chips, I've made these with white chocolate chips and cranberries, and they were just as irresistible.

strawberry rhubarb streusel crumb pie

Serves 8-10

The first time I ever tasted a rhubarb pie was in Cortland, New York. My friend, Jimmy, and I drove upstate, to what was considered "the country," to see his mother. She served us a rhubarb pie with a slice of cheddar cheese on it, and I thought she was crazy. (Turns out it's pretty good that way.) Ever since then, rhubarb pie has been one of my favorites. Bake it at home for a taste of country kitchen goodness.

1 rolled refrigerated pie crust (from a 14.1-ounce package)

3 cups sliced strawberries

2 cups sliced frozen rhubarb, thawed and drained well

½ cup granulated sugar

¼ cup all-purpose flour

1 tablespoon butter, melted

Streusel Topping

1 cup all-purpose flour

½ cup brown sugar

1 stick cold butter, cut into ½-inch cubes

❀ Preheat oven to 375 degrees F. Unroll pie crust, press into a 9-inch deep dish pie plate, and flute edges.

❀ In a large bowl, combine strawberries, rhubarb, and sugar; mix well until the sugar is dissolved. Add ¼ cup flour and 1 tablespoon melted butter; mix well and spoon into the pie crust.

❀ In a medium bowl, combine Streusel Topping ingredients. Mix well, and sprinkle topping over the strawberry rhubarb mixture.

❀ Bake 45 to 50 minutes or until the streusel is golden and the filling is bubbly. Allow to cool before serving, or chill until ready to serve

Chef Tony's Tip: Since rhubarb has a rather short season, I suggest using frozen rhubarb, which is available year-round. That way, you can make this pie any time of the year.

black-bottom georgia pecan pie

Serves 8-10

This is the perfect dessert for Thanksgiving or any time you're craving a really decadent slice of pie. Since I'm such a fan of pecan pie, and you already know how I feel about brownies (see page 199), I came up with this twist on a classic. My pecan pie has a fudgy, brownie-like bottom and plenty of buttery pecans to keep me happy. Serve it with a big scoop of ice cream, and expect no leftovers.

1 rolled refrigerated pie crust (from a 14.1-ounce package)

6 tablespoons butter

½ cup bittersweet chocolate chips

1-½ cups pecan halves, divided

1 cup corn syrup

4 eggs

1 cup light brown sugar

1 teaspoon vanilla extract

¼ teaspoon salt

✳ Preheat oven to 350 degrees F. Unroll pie crust, press into a 9-inch pie plate, and flute edges; set aside.

✳ In a small saucepan over low heat, melt butter and chocolate chips, stirring until smooth; let cool slightly. Chop ½ cup pecans and set aside.

✳ Meanwhile, in a large bowl, whisk corn syrup, eggs, brown sugar, vanilla, and salt. Stir the chocolate mixture into the corn syrup mixture, along with the ½ cup chopped pecans until thoroughly combined. Pour the mixture into the pie crust.

✳ Arrange the remaining pecan halves over the filling, as shown. Bake 40 to 45 minutes or until the filling is no longer jiggly in the center. Let cool completely before serving.

key lime tartlets

Makes 12

I tried my first key lime pie on my first visit to Florida. The lady who made it for me was originally from one of the Caribbean islands, but she had spent some time in the Florida Keys. After just a few bites, I was hooked. In fact, I thought it was so good that I felt inspired to make it myself. Now, when I need a ray of sunshine, I make these mini-sized versions at home.

1 cup finely crushed vanilla wafer cookies

1 teaspoon sugar

2 tablespoons butter, melted

3 egg yolks

1-½ teaspoons grated lime zest

1 (14-ounce) can sweetened condensed milk

⅔ cup key lime juice (see Tip)

Whipped cream and lime wedges for topping

✳ Preheat oven to 350 degrees F. Line 12 muffin cups with paper liners.

✳ In a medium bowl combine cookie crumbs, sugar, and butter; mix well, then press the mixture evenly into the bottom of the paper liners, using your fingertips.

✳ In a medium bowl, using an electric mixer on medium speed, beat egg yolks and lime zest for 2 to 3 minutes or until fluffy. Gradually add sweetened condensed milk and continue beating 3 to 4 minutes until it's well mixed. Reduce speed to low and gradually beat in lime juice just until it's combined. Pour filling into muffin cups.

✳ Bake 10 minutes or until the centers are firm. Remove from oven and let cool on a wire rack, then cover and chill at least 2 hours. Before serving, remove the paper liners; top with whipped cream and lime wedges.

Chef Tony's Tip: Key lime juice should be next to the regular lime juice in your supermarket. If you don't see it there, it may be hiding with the bar mixers. If all else fails, you could use regular lime juice too.

secret ingredient fabulous flan

Serves 12-14

If you've made flan before, you're probably going to look at the cream cheese in the ingredients and say, "that doesn't belong there," but trust me, it does. This recipe was shared with me by a Spanish woman whom I met at a Christmas party at our church in Brooklyn. She told me that the secret to making a flan that's a little firmer, but still light, is to use cream cheese. I just wanna dive in and live in this dessert.

1-¾ cups sugar, divided

1 (8-ounce) package cream cheese, cut into cubes, softened

1 (12-ounce) can evaporated milk

5 eggs

1-½ teaspoons vanilla extract

✳ Preheat oven to 350 degrees F.

✳ In a small skillet over medium heat, cook ¾ cup sugar until melted and golden, stirring constantly. Immediately pour melted sugar into a 9-inch cake pan or pie plate, tilting it side-to-side until the melted sugar evenly covers the bottom.

✳ In a blender, combine cream cheese and evaporated milk; blend until smooth. Add remaining 1 cup sugar, the eggs, and vanilla, and blend until thoroughly combined. Pour mixture over caramelized sugar in pan.

✳ Place the cake pan in a large roasting pan. Pour just enough hot water into the roasting pan to go halfway up the sides of the cake pan.

✳ Bake 55 to 60 minutes or until a knife inserted in center comes out clean. Cool slightly, then remove flan from hot water bath and allow it to cool for 1 hour. Cover and chill 8 hours or overnight.

✳ Just before serving, run a knife around the edge of the pan to loosen the flan. Invert the flan onto a rimmed serving platter and enjoy.

Chef Tony's Tip: Make sure you use a serving platter with a deep lip, otherwise the caramelized syrup will ooze all over the place, and it would be a real shame to waste it!

crumbly shortbread cookies

Makes 3 dozen

If you like your cookies crumbly, buttery, and a little nutty, then you'll love these shortbread cookies. I've seen some form of these cookies served at weddings, parties, and holiday occasions, and they're always popular. So go ahead and add these to your next cookie platter, then watch them disappear!

2 sticks butter, softened

⅓ cup granulated sugar

2 teaspoons vanilla extract

2 teaspoons water

2 cups all-purpose flour

1 cup finely chopped pecans

½ cup powdered sugar

❋ Preheat oven to 325 degrees F.

❋ In a large bowl using an electric mixer on medium-high speed, cream butter and granulated sugar until fluffy. Add vanilla and water; beat well. With a wooden spoon, stir in flour and pecans.

❋ Shape into 1-inch balls and place about 1-inch apart on ungreased baking sheets.

❋ Bake 20 to 25 minutes or until the bottoms of the cookies are light golden. Remove to wire racks to cool completely.

❋ Place powdered sugar in a plastic storage bag; add a few cookies at a time and shake gently until completely coated. Store in an airtight container until ready to serve.

Chef Tony's Tip: You don't want to store these in the refrigerator because if you do, the powdered sugar will start to "melt" off of them.

peanut butter pretzel balls

Makes 2 dozen

Where are all my peanut butter lovers? I hope you're one of them, because this recipe is for anybody who's ever eaten peanut butter right out of the jar. These no-bake pretzel balls are made with one of the world's greatest combinations - peanut butter and chocolate, so it's no wonder they're addictive!

1 cup peanut butter

1 cup powdered sugar

1 tablespoon butter, softened

1 cup crushed pretzels

1 cup semisweet chocolate chips

1 teaspoon shortening

✳ Line a rimmed baking sheet with wax paper.

✳ In a medium bowl, stir together peanut butter, powdered sugar, butter, and pretzels. Roll into 1-inch balls and arrange on the lined baking sheet. Freeze 30 minutes or until firm.

✳ In a small, microwave-safe bowl, microwave chocolate chips and shortening in 30 second intervals, stirring until the chocolate is melted and smooth. Place in a plastic bag that has one corner snipped. Drizzle chocolate mixture over pretzel bites in a random fashion. Refrigerate until set. When chilled, enjoy.

chocolate chunk macadamia nut cookies

Makes a baker's dozen (13)

These are just like the ones Mom used to make; puffy, chocolaty, and nutty. I loved these cookies so much growing up, that I never stopped making them. Plus, there's something about sharing these big, sink-your-teeth-into cookies with friends and family that makes any moment just a little bit more special. I hope these cookies bring you and your loved ones together too.

1 stick butter, melted

1 egg

1-½ teaspoons vanilla extract

¾ cup sugar

1-½ cups all-purpose flour

½ teaspoon baking soda

½ teaspoon salt

¾ cup coarsely chopped macadamia nuts

1 cup semisweet chocolate chunks

✳ Preheat oven to 375 degrees F. Coat baking sheets with cooking spray.

✳ In a large bowl, combine butter, egg, vanilla, and sugar; mix well. Stir in flour, baking soda, and salt. Add nuts and chocolate chunks; mix well. Refrigerate dough 15 minutes.

✳ Drop 13 equal mounds onto the baking sheets, about 2 inches apart.

✳ Bake 13 to 15 minutes or until edges are brown. Let cool 5 minutes, then remove to a wire rack to cool completely. Enjoy right away or store these in an airtight container.

Chef Tony's Tip: My mom taught me that in order to have a cookie that you can really bite into, the mounds of dough need to be more like a scoop since they'll flatten slightly as they bake.

limoncello mousse with dippers

Serves 6

A taste of the homeland! If Sicily hopped on a plane and took a flight to America, it'd bring along this dessert right here. Light, flavorful, and with just the right amount of tartness to it, this mousse is going to rock your world. It's a great dessert to make for fancier occasions too, since it's easy, but has a gourmet taste and a fancy look to it.

1 (8-ounce) container mascarpone cheese

¾ cup powdered sugar

5 tablespoons limoncello liqueur

1 teaspoon lemon zest

1 cup heavy cream

12 ladyfingers (the hard kind)

½ (6-ounce) package white baking bar, shaved

✳ In a large bowl using an electric mixer on medium-high speed, beat mascarpone cheese and powdered sugar until creamy. Add limoncello liqueur and lemon zest; mix until combined.

✳ In a medium bowl, whip heavy cream until stiff peaks form. Gently fold the whipped cream into the cheese mixture until thoroughly combined. Spoon the mixture into 6 parfait glasses or a serving bowl. Cover and chill for at least 1 hour.

✳ When it's time for dessert, serve these with a couple of ladyfingers for dipping. Then finish each one with some shaved white chocolate.

Chef Tony's Tip: save the rest of the white chocolate bar that you don't use for the next time you make this dessert.

recipes in alphabetical order

recipes in alphabetical order

recipes by category

recipes by category

recipes by category

recipes by category